OUT OF HIS HEAD:

The Sound of Phil Spector

OUT OF HIS HEAD:

THE SOUND OF PHIL SPECTOR

Richard Williams

/ |

OUTERBRIDGE & LAZARD, INC.

New York
Distributed by E. P. Dutton & Co.

Standard Book Number: 0–87690–067–8
Library of Congress Catalog Number: 71–190491
Copyright ☉ 1972 Richard Williams
First published in the United States of America
  in 1972
Printed in the United States of America
All rights reserved including the right of reproduction
  in whole or in part in any form.

Design: Ellen Seham
        David E. Seham Associates

Out of His Head is one of a number of books
  being published by Outerbridge & Lazard, Inc.
  selected and under the general editorial direction of
  Charlie Gillett, author of *The Sound of the City*.

Photographs on pages 6 and 10 by Iain Macmillan.
Photographs on pages 45, 63, 84, 91, 98, and 106 reproduced by
  kind permission of the *Melody Maker*.

MUS.
92
Spector, P.

OUTERBRIDGE & LAZARD, INC.

200 W. 72 Street New York 10023

CONTENTS

1

ACKNOWLEDGMENTS, ETC.

IT WOULD NOT HAVE BEEN POSSIBLE TO WRITE this book without help, advice, and information from many sources, most of whom didn't know me from Adam before I rang up and said: "I'm writing a book about Phil Spector. Can you tell me. . . ."

So my thanks go to Danny Davis, Jeff Barry, Mike Stoller, Paul Case, Lou Adler, Tony Hall, Bill Millar, Dave Stein, Bob (at the House of Oldies), Steve Flam (of *Bim Bam Boom* magazine), Bob Richardson, James Hamilton, Janet Martin, Peter Eden, Clive Woods, Pat Pretty, George Brand, Ian Whitcomb, Al Steckler, May Pang, Iain Macmillan, John and Yoko, Phil and Ronnie Spector, and, particularly, to Tony Orlando—a true Spector freak. Special gratitude to Charlie Gillett, whose encouragement was invaluable, and to my wife, Alison. All these people demonstrated patience and enthusiasm far beyond the call of duty.

This book is respectfully dedicated to the memory of Frankie Lymon.

Chapter 1, AND SO THIS IS CHRISTMAS, is adapted from a longer piece which first appeared in the *Melody Maker*. It is reprinted by kind permission of the Editor, Ray Coleman.

OUT OF HIS HEAD:

The Sound of Phil Spector

1

AND SO THIS IS CHRISTMAS
"I know something about Christmas records, y'know...."

UP ON THE 17TH FLOOR OF THE ST. REGIS HOTEL in New York City, John Lennon wades on his hands and knees through a pile of Presley singles. Their bright red labels litter the deep-pile carpet, forming a river which flows under the big unmade bed. He sorts them out into the good, the bad, and the ugly, with the idea of putting the former on a jukebox in his new loft in Greenwich Village.

It's the afternoon of Thursday, October 28, 1971. John is talking about his plans to hit the road with the Plastic Ono Band in the next few months. "I've got a lot to learn," he sighs. "It's been seven years, you know . . . but it's important to get the band on the road, to get tight. It's been fun just turning up at odd gigs like Toronto and the Lyceum and the Fillmore, but I'm sick of having to sing 'Blue Suede Shoes' because we haven't rehearsed anything else."

The band will have as a nucleus himself on rhythm guitar and vocals, Yoko, Nicky Hopkins on piano, Klaus Voorman on bass, and Jim Keltner on drums. With a bit of luck, he adds, Phil Spector will be there singing and playing guitar, on stage for the first time since the Teddy Bears hit the road in 1959.

John hopes to turn the new troupe into a circus-cum-carnival, with street theatre groups and bands from wherever the troupe is playing taking part. John plans to send Yippie leader Jerry Rubin on ahead of the main caravan to organize.

Scratching his head, undecided over how to assign "Love Me Tender", he starts talking about his own songs, and how he pinches bits from favorite old rock and roll numbers. Finally he throws "Love Me Tender" onto the "wanted" pile, picks up his guitar, and sings a new one about Chuck Berry and Bo Diddley. The middle-eight, he points out, is pinched from "Quarter To Three" by U. S. Bonds, which he heard on the radio the previous day.

He and the Plastic Ono Band are recording a song that very night for their special Christmas single. It's called "Happy Christmas (War Is Over)." "The 'War Is Over' bit's in brackets, like the old American records," says John. When John first played it to Spector, the producer commented straight off that the tune was a direct lift from "I Love How You Love Me," Phil's 1961 hit with the Paris Sisters.

John rolls back into bed to get some kip before the session. It's now around three o'clock in the afternoon, and he's got four hours to catch up on the sleep he lost last night while out conferring with Rubin.

‽

Four hours and ten minutes later, John sits with his jumbo guitar on the fringed carpet of the Record Plant, a small, comfortable studio on West 44th Street between 8th and 9th Avenues. He is teaching the chords of "Happy Christmas" to the five young acoustic guitarists who surround him.

Why all those rhythm guitarists? Well, Spector had called the previous day from his office on the West Coast wanting to know who was playing on the session. John's assistant told him there'd be John, Yoko, Nicky, Klaus, and Keltner. Spector exploded. "Listen . . . I want five rhythm guitars. And if it's a Christmas record, get me some percussion . . . bells, celeste, chimes. . . ."

Most of the guitarists are young and inexperienced friends of a boy John met in a New York music shop, but among them is Hugh McCracken, the brilliant session musician who played on McCartney's *Ram* album. John doesn't know this yet however. He asks their names. "Chris." "Stu." "Teddy." "Hugh." John turns to Yoko. "Hey, Hugh looks like Ivan, doesn't he? Hugh, you look just like an old mate of mine from school . . . a cross between him and Paul."

There's a little break, while everyone gets up to stretch limbs. Somebody tells John about Hugh's past accomplishments. John laughs, and can't resist a crack. "Oh, so you were just auditioning on *Ram*, were you? Yeah, 'e said you were all right." With that, what tension there had been among the younger musicians disappears.

They get back to learning the tune and feel of the song. "Just pretend it's Christmas," John exhorts them. "I'm Jewish," says one. "Well pretend it's your birthday then."

Suddenly there's a little flurry at the entrance. It's Spector, just in from the Coast, with big shades and neatly-pressed denims. Over his left breast rests a red and white button bearing the legend "Back to MONO." The button has the guys in the booth breaking up. But it's serious.

Within seconds the session switches from playtime to worktime. It takes Spector roughly one minute to transform the guitars on the control room's monitor speakers from a happy rabble into a brilliant, cutting wash of color. And they aren't even miked properly yet.

"Play that back to 'em," Phil tells Roy, the engineer. "It'll get 'em relaxed." It does. During the playback Phil enters the studio and dances with John, arms around each other's shoulders.

They run through the changes again, with Nicky on piano this time. Spector leans down to the intercom, presses a little green button, and commands: "Guitars, play the basic rhythm. Don't play anything else, nothing across the beat. Just keep it simple and play together. Nicky, I'd like to hear more of that in octaves in the right hand . . . makes it more dramatic." John cranes towards his guitar mike and shouts: "Phil, don't dictate to 'em yet. Let's get comfortable first." "Okay," answers Phil, visibly trying to contain his energy.

Spector is already into the groove. He is thinking not just of sound, but of arrangement and drama—production. His weird little head is taking the simple guitar chords and molding, blending, and transforming them—his old pattern. Well ahead of everyone, even Lennon, he imagines the sound coming out of a million, two-inch transistor speakers.

At this point they add bass and drums. Keltner settles behind his kit into a small fenced-off area on one side. One of the rhythm guitarists is moved over to bass—Klaus's flight from Germany has been delayed and he's going to miss the session, but the group can't wait.

They run the tune down a few more times all together. It's sounding good, the tapes are spinning. Every so often they all crowd into the booth to hear a playback.

John: "I like the ones that sound like *records*...."

"... before you've made 'em," Phil finishes the sentence for him. It's obvious that they're a fine double act.

Almost imperceptibly they slip into takes. During the third complete take the sound really begins to lift off. Phil sits in the center of the board, constantly spitting instructions to the engineer beside him. The take is sounding real good now, and Phil's voice gets louder: "More echo on the piano, Roy ... more echo ... more ... more

Spector supervises session musicians at the recording session for the Plastic Ono Band's "Happy Xmas" single.

. . . MORE ECHO, C'MON! That's it! Beautiful!"

During the second chorus he stands up. The thick, soundproof window between the booth and the big room is split into three, like an old-fashioned car windscreen. Phil's triple reflection upon the glass looms large and surreal across the picture of the musicians beyond the window. The illusion presents an exact metaphor of the session.

Spector's arms are spread now, windmilling with the beat. As the climax approaches he stares over the heads of the guitarists straight into Keltner's eyes and wills him to lay into his tom-toms, to explode on the fills. Keltner grimaces and strains to oblige—the take ends in a blaze of glory. *"Great!"* Phil screams. That's it, and everyone knows it.

The overdubs start, and again the Spector magic becomes overwhelmingly apparent. At John's suggestion, they begin with guitars on a mandolin-like line which wanders behind the verse. Inside ten minutes, the guitars are finished and on the track.

They try out all sorts of percussive effects, finally settling on Nicky to play chimes and glockenspiel, while Keltner adds a jangling four-to-the-bar with a handy set of sleighbells. "How can you make a record called 'Happy Christmas' without bells?" Phil had asked rhetorically. Now he smiles and mutters on the side: "I know something about Christmas records, y'know."

Instantly, a flashback to Philles LP405, *A Christmas Gift To You*—after that, Phil probably knew more about making Christmas records than Sauter and Finegan, whose orchestral arrangement of "Sleigh Ride" was a favorite Christmas record of the early Fifties.

It's vocal time, so John and Yoko clap on the headphones and start practicing, while Phil has the engineer run the track for them. John sounds wheezy and is unable to hit the high notes. Phil shouts through the talkback: "Yoko's outsinging you, John." He flips off the mike, shakes his head in disapproval: "He's smoking his ass off while he's singing." Bobby Hatfield would never have got away with it, but then this *is* John Lennon, after all.

Finally, with the aid of tactful prods in the back, John gets Yoko to come in at all the right places. Phil gets the correct echo on the voices, and they lay it down.

Now they start talking about what to do with the strings and kiddie's choir, scheduled for overdubbing during the next few days. Phil thinks it'd be a good idea to have the violins play "Silent Night" over the fade, while John suggests a cello figure for the chorus.

Once again, they do a rough remix. But it's 4 a.m., time for everyone to go home. Phil and the Lennons leave in their black chauffeured Caddies.

Three hours later, one of the onlookers at the session turns over in his sleep and wakes up. He finds himself singing:

"War is over . . . if you want it . . . war is over now."

ɣ

The following night, the band runs through Yoko's composition "Snow Is Falling," the B side of the new single. The song is five years old, the first song she showed John when they got together. At last she's getting the chance to record it.

Phil is there with his brother-in-law Joe, a short, thick-set man whose Italian-American accent could be cut with a switchblade. Joe, in the grand tradition of Phil's "assistants," stands by the wall of the booth all night, not saying a word, moving only when Phil mutters for the Scotch. Joe then rummages in a blue flight bag for the bottle of J & B, and mixes the drink with water in a borrowed glass. Phil gets very annoyed when they run out of ice. Joe gets worried, but stays good-natured, wandering around murmuring "I gotta find da ice." Somehow he always does.

Back in the studio there's an argument in progress. John and Yoko can't agree on the tempo. "I'm not gonna play on this," says John, who'd been plucking out lines on Creedence-ish reverb guitar.

"I asked you to play organ," says Yoko. "I've been asking you to do that all along."

John returns to the booth, where Phil greets him with: "I thought this was supposed to be a light thing." It was, John agrees, "but she says 'faster' and they all get to rocking like shit."

Yoko tells Nicky to play lighter on the intro: "Pretend that it's snowing . . . that snow is melting on your fingertips. Not that banging."

Nicky gets it right the next time, while Klaus and Hugh McCracken, who has been invited back, work out little runs and licks reminiscent of Curtis Mayfield's "People Get Ready."

Klaus and Yoko are into a shouting match over the placement of chords at the end of the song. Klaus gets up, unstraps his bass, and appears ready to walk out. But John placates both of them, and they try it again—this time successfully. They try a take, and get a good one almost immediately.

John: "Fantastic. . . ."
Phil: "Great, great tape echo. . . ."
Yoko: "How was my voice?"
Phil: "Great . . . lots of tape echo. . . ."

The track sounds simple and pretty enough as is, but within minutes they talk about adding organ, chimes,

Spector with John and Yoko, listening to playbacks.

more guitar, and even sound effects. What they want is the sound of a celeste, but they haven't got one. The engineers set to work on getting a celeste sound out of the electric piano. As they're working, Nicky and Hugh and Keltner start to play a medium blues.

"Oh-oh," says Phil. "They've started jamming, and we'll never get anything done. Let's put a stop to *that.*" He moves to the connecting door, but Yoko pre-empts him.

"STOP JAMMING!" she screams, almost bursting the speakers. The musicians stop as one man, right in mid-eighthnote.

Yoko is obviously more than a little tense. She confides her belief that the musicians don't take her songs as seriously as she'd like. But this is a very good song, no doubt about it. It also sounds extremely commercial—she flutters her hands with delight when, after the overdubs, someone says it sounds more like a Top Five smash than a B side.

But they haven't finished yet. They haven't forgotten about the sound effects. One of the engineers digs out the standard effects album that all studios keep for such occasions. They decide to open and close the track with the sound of "Feet in the snow" superimposed on "Strong wind."

The lights are turned off for the final playback. It's really magical: "Listen . . . the snow is falling everywhere."

Leaving the studio is a shock—those soft, white flakes aren't drifting down through chill night air. It's quite warm out, actually.

ƒ

Sunday afternoon at the studio they start early because the choir is there, and the choir has to be in bed early.

The choir consists of about 30 black kids, from around age four to age twelve, plus four nubile teens whom John instantly dubs "The Supremes." A few of the kids' mothers shush and cluck around the studio, making sure that ribbon-bows aren't crooked.

John and Yoko teach the kids the tune by example and from words on a blackboard. After only a few tries the kids have got it, and the voices are superimposed on the already mixed track. But Phil now insists the kids do it one more time. He dubs the new recording on top—there are now 60 voices on the record.

Apart from the strings it's all over, so the Lennons, the Supremes, the mothers, the kids, the band, the engineers, the studio secretary, Phil, and the unwilling Joe gather round to pose for a possible cover picture. A green plastic Christmas tree with dangling lights, specially bought for the occasion, towers above the group.

The photographer is a little slow. He can't seem to fit everyone into the frame, so Phil takes over. "C'mon Iain . . . when I shout 'ONE TWO THREE', everybody shout 'HAPPY CHRISTMAS' and you take the picture. Right? ONE TWO THREE (HAPPY CHRISTMAS) ONE TWO THREE (HAPPY CHRISTMAS) ONE TWO THREE (HAPPY CHRISTMAS). Okay Iain, you got it."

Shortly after midnight, two black Cadillacs pull away from the curb outside the Record Plant and swing into 8th Avenue. They travel one block in convoy, before the first car, carrying John and Yoko, swings off to the left into 45th Street.

The second car carries on down 8th. The partition is shut. Sitting right in the middle of the wide rear seat, is a small figure with long, sculptured hair and goggle-shaped shades.

Above his left breast is a button. It says: "Back to MONO." That's where the Caddy is going.

2

PRODUCED BY PHIL SPECTOR
"My dream was to invent the word 'producer'...."

ONE OF THE MOST CELEBRATED MOMENTS IN late-Sixties rock comes at the beginning of "To Be Alone With You" on Bob Dylan's *Nashville Skyline* album. As the guitars begin to strum, Dylan drawls, "Is it rolling, Bob?"

"Bob" is Bob Johnston, Dylan's producer. With that single question Dylan brings to our attention Johnston's role in the singer's recording career. The producer is here acknowledged as a crucial part of the whole undertaking—as necessary as the tape machines, microphones, and instruments . . . almost as important as the singer himself.

By the end of the Sixties, most rock fans could give you the names of any number of important producers: Jimmy Miller (with the Rolling Stones), George Martin (with the Beatles), Kit Lambert (with the Who), the Holland brothers and Lamont Dozier (with Motown's Four Tops and the Supremes), and so on. It was important to know that Stephen Stills produced the Crosby, Stills, Nash and Young albums, and that Bob Krasnow's production techniques were a crucial factor in the sound of Captain Beefheart's *Strictly Personal* album. Production methods had an immense influence on the aesthetics of the music in question.

It is pure speculation, and almost certainly untrue, to say that none of this would have happened without Phil Spector. But it's equally certain that it was he, single handed, who turned the producer from an obscure back-room boy whose name was of little or no importance to the average record buyer, into a figure parallel with the great movie directors. The comparison is in fact valid. Just as we not only ask "Have you seen the new Brando movie?" but also "Have you seen the new Losey?", so in the mid-Sixties did we ask, "Have you heard the new Spector single?" neglecting, probably, to add whether the singers on the record were the Crystals, the Ronettes, or the Righteous Brothers.

Of course there were producers before Phil Spector, important men who helped mold the way music reached our ears. Some, like John Hammond, played a vital role in the history of popular music, by helping performers of real talent to overcome neglect and racial barriers. Beginning in 1931, Hammond started bringing to public attention jazz artists like Count Basie, Billie Holiday, Lester Young, Mildred Bailey, and Lionel Hampton. In fact it was he who persuaded Benny Goodman to hire the pianist Teddy Wilson—the first time a black musician was able to join a "name" band. It was a giant step. Hammond maintaned his track record after the war: while with Columbia Records he brought both Aretha Franklin and Bob Dylan to the label.

As a record producer, Hammond assumed the standard function of middleman between the artist and the engineer. He made sure that the material selected was suitable, that a good sound was obtained on the tape, and that all concerned were happy with the environment and results. He might have suggestions such as bringing certain musicians together for a date, but his aesthetic control did not extend beyond that. Which was how he wanted it, since his only desire was to allow musicians to place their particular talents on tape in the optimum circumstances. It is significant that after Aretha was taken from under Hammond's wing, where she had been increasingly successful with Blues and Gospel material, she was forced to record supposedly commercial pop songs and became a dismal failure. Some years later she joined Atlantic, where producer Jerry Wexler reverted to Hammond's pattern, with brilliant success, both artistic and commercial.

Another way of approaching a producer's work was presented by George Goldner, one of the great rock and roll producers of the Fifties. In '53 Goldner formed the Gee label—to which were added later Rama, Gone, End, and Goldisc. He specialized in street-corner groups, mostly black or Puerto Rican, who hung around the poor areas of New York, harmonizing endlessly either on current favorites or their own compositions. These groups were in the process of inventing a whole new sound. Goldner capitalized on it by going out, grabbing them up, pulling them into his recording studio, and cutting a couple of sides for which he'd pay them a few dollars. Rarely were these records anything more than regional hits around New York (how many people elsewhere remember the Heartbeats, the Wrens, or the Harptones?), but occasionally sales were so big that a record would reach the national charts, from where radio stations around the country would start picking it up. This happened to 13-year-old Frankie

Lymon and his group, the Teenagers. Goldner cut a record with them called "Why Do Fools Fall In Love", a song written by Lymon. In the early part of 1956 the recording sold a million copies, reaching number seven on the national chart.

Goldner also launched Little Anthony and the Imperials on the End label, but his first really big recording (some have called it the first real rock and roll record) was "Gee," by the Crows—the sound which former Creedence Clearwater guitarist Tom Fogerty has cited as the key which first turned him on to the potential power of pop music.

As a producer in the later sense of the term, Goldner was nothing. It is likely, as English writer Bill Miller has suggested, that Goldner persuaded his black groups to sweeten their delivery for the huge white market, but, like Hammond, he was more of an organizer than a creator. Unlike Hammond though, he was a hustler, and that, to some extent, is how he came to influence Spector. Goldner knew how to get his records played on the radio—and there's no denying that he extracted the maximum possible percentage for himself. For instance, he gave himself a co-authorship credit on "Why Do Fools Fall In Love," thus taking for himself half the composer royalties. In addition he organized a tie-up with the large Roulette complex, and thus ensured that his records were exposed to the best advantage and widest distribution.

It was that commercial ability that Spector admired almost as much as he loved the sounds that Goldner's groups made. It was a different kind of "producing," which made its influence felt when Phil finally came to form his own independent record company, Philles, in 1961. Goldner had made the industry work for him, and that's what Spector set out to emulate.

Spector's real spiritual ancestor, however, was Sam Phillips, owner of Sun Records in Memphis. It was Phillips who cut Elvis Presley's first and greatest records: "That's All Right," "Mystery Train," "Baby Let's Play House," "You're A Heartbreaker," and so on—all characterized by an innovative use of tape-echo. Instead of producing the cavernous, bathroomy effect obtained by the over-lavish use of echo chamber so beloved of contemporary producers, Phillips' method gave the records a larger-than-life quality. The snare drum and string bass snapped in unison. This "presence" gave the records an indefinable lift and vitality. It didn't just happen on Presley's records, either; Phillips did the same with Jerry Lee Lewis on "Whole Lotta Shakin' Going On" and "Great Balls of Fire," and on lesser known classics like Warren Smith's "Rock and Roll Ruby." The sound affected a whole generation, and it turned Spector around.

These, then, were the three basic types of producer before Spector came along: the more or less altruistic organizer, the shrewd businessman, and the studio innovator. Spector took all three, rolled them into one, added his own genius, and created a totally new concept: the producer as overall director. In the process he put out a group of the most memorable records in all of pop music.

He took control of everything. He picked the bands, wrote or chose the material, supervised the arrangements, told the singers how to phrase, masterminded all phases of the recording process, and released the result on his own label, a label with no affiliation with any of the supposedly all-powerful major record companies. He introduced many innovations: by concentrating all his efforts on one record at a time, he avoided the wasteful scattershot policy of the majors; by bringing the technique of overdubbing to a new peak, he created a sound never heard before, a sound which came to be known as The Spector Sound throughout the world's recording industry.

He also revolutionized the industry's attitude to youth. Previously, older men like Alan Freed, Dick Clark, Goldner, and the presidents of the major labels had exerted total control over the pop youth culture. Kids made the music, but they had no say in what happened after it got onto the tape, and they rarely saw much of the money. Because of this, they often fell back into obscurity after their brief glimpse of limelight, and often their lives (like that of Frankie Lymon) ended in squalid tragedy. The kids made it and the kids bought it, but it was the "cigar-chomping fatties" who first took the cream, and then the milk, and finally threw the empty bottle into the trash can.

Spector set out to change all that. He fought the system through his own company. To make the changes he had to succeed, succeed, and succeed again. At 21 years of age even one failure would have been too costly. It would have enabled the fatties to smirk and tell themselves that the kids couldn't handle it after all; that they actually *needed* the older guys to take care of business for them. But Spector did succeed, for more than four straight years. Eventually the industry got him, its rage no longer containable, but while he was hot he was always sowing the seeds for a new self-determination, the birthright now demanded by every rock musician. These days you won't find a George Goldner telling Neil Young or John Fogerty what to do to get a hit record (of course this is not *necessarily* a good thing for all the Neil Youngs and John Fogertys).

Spector's musical influence has been immense, both in general and in specific areas. Remember "I Got You Babe," by Sonny and Cher? That record and that group happened because Sonny Bono wanted to *be* Phil Spector. So did Andrew Oldham, the Rolling Stones' first producer: the sound and style of the early Stones owes a great debt to Spector, as does the studio sound of the Beach Boys as developed by Brian Wilson. The scale of Spector's efforts prompted Wilson to investigate the technical resources at his command; it is likely that, had there not been a Phil Spector, there would not have been a "Good Vibrations" either.

Neither would there have been a Shadow Morton. Not one of the best known producers, Morton nevertheless came up with some of the most interesting records of the middle and late Sixties, the epic "Leader of The Pack" by the Shangri-Las, and the first album by Vanilla Fudge, one of rock's great testaments.

All these men and their records have altered the face of pop. It can be said that they changed it from a performing art into an art which could exist only inside a recording studio, making possible such artifacts as the Beatles' "A Day In The Life," or the Four Tops' "Reach Out, I'll Be There."

Surely no greater tribute could be paid to Spector's giant importance than his appointment early in 1970 as virtual working head of the record division of Apple. Spector owns the ultimate power of veto over whatever goes out on the label. Since 1970 he has produced everything by John Lennon and George Harrison, thus fitting effortlessly into the fastest company in the entire rock world. And he looks so *right* there; other producers could give the ex-Beatles' records an adequate sound, and could pander to their whims in the studio, but only Spector could stand with them on an equal footing, not fearing to lend his own ideas for the one goal of better music. Which, as we shall see, is what he was (almost) always about.

3

TO KNOW HIM IS TO LOVE HIM
"I was into that at
a very early age...."

PHIL SPECTOR WAS BORN IN THE BRONX ON December 26, 1940, into an "average lower middle class" family. His father died when Spector was nine. Three years later his mother Bertha, a very strong personality, took the family off to live in California, which was already beginning to look like America's own Promised Land, with booming job opportunities and, at that time, a seemingly endless supply of fresh air.

In high school Phil started to become interested in music. He learned to play piano, guitar, drums, and French horn, and started listening hard to what was going on around him. What he heard was the harsh, raunchy sound of Rhythm and Blues—and in particular the records produced by a duo called Jerry Leiber and Mike Stoller.

Leiber and Stoller had been writing together since the late Forties. They were white, but they understood black music—particularly Leiber, who'd been brought up in a ghetto area and picked up first hand the vernacular and speech rhythms of black people.

Based in Los Angeles, Jerry and Mike cut the original version of "Hound Dog" with Willie Mae Thornton in 1952. When Elvis Presley picked up the song in 1956 and made it into a number one hit, Presley decided to find out who the writers were. His management contacted

Leiber and Stoller, who in turn began to churn out a succession of great songs for Presley: "Jailhouse Rock," "King Creole," "I Want To Be Free," and "Baby I Don't Care," for instance.

But Leiber and Stoller's best records, and the ones which probably influenced Spector most, were sung by a group called the Coasters on the Spark label. Leiber and Stoller had set up Spark in association with Lester Sill, an energetic and effective promotion man for the R & B label Modern, who had provided the songwriters with their entrée into the Los Angeles music business, and who also managed the Coasters.

The duo, however, soon tired of the hassles of manufacturing and shipping their own records, and the troubles of getting airplay outside the ghetto areas of Los Angeles and San Francisco. So they signed a deal with Atlantic Records, whereby Atlantic bought all the Spark masters and signed Leiber and Stoller as staff producers.

Jerry and Mike formed the Coasters from two ex-Robins and two others. Between '56 and '59 they produced a string of classics on Atlantic with the new group: "Young Blood," "Searchin'," "Yakety Yak," "Charlie Brown," "Poison Ivy," and so on. They became one of the three or four top black vocal groups. Atlantic's machine had given them the "push" on a national scale which Spark couldn't muster.

It was only natural that the paths of Leiber, Stoller, and Spector, should converge in later years. As Spector would in the Sixties, Leiber and Stoller used the black singers as tools, manipulating their every musical move with infinite care in order to achieve exactly the effect that they, the producers, had heard. The singers really didn't have much to do with it. All they contributed was the individuality and emotional color of their voices, for even their phrasing was minutely controlled.

The Coaster's records have been described as "situation comedies," each one a tight little slab of humorous realism. Take "Down In Mexico," for example. Leiber and Stoller spare no pains to build up a little sound picture of a sleazy Mexican cafe using Spanish guitar, imaginative percussion, and very greasy tenor sax. The producers themselves have stated that they spent hours at rehearsal and in the studio with the group in order to get the timing of the comedy lines exactly right. Two passages of "Down In Mexico" provide particular evidence of careful planning: the middle section, where the singer eases out his words referring to the entrance of a Spanish dancer over a stark tom-tom beat; and the ending, where one of the group starts talking in a hilarious quasi-Mexican accent.

But the crucial effect is one of spontaneity. Despite all the care lavished on the record, the singers still sound stoned out of their minds, while the band sounds no better than any ordinary cabaret outfit. This was what Spector was later to achieve, "spontaneous" excitement through precise preplanning—like Leiber and Stoller he learned how to harness the talents of the black singers and mold them into something acceptable to white audiences as well.

The Coasters' hits are still the finest pop comedy records ever made, and they must have exerted a strong pull on the young Spector. But his interest didn't end simply with listening and digging.

"Everybody sort of suspected what I was going to be," he says. "There was this game called stickball, where you'd hit the ball and run around the base, and whenever we'd be playing the joke was, 'You be pitcher and you be hitter and Phil, you produce the game.' Even then, in 1955 or '54, it was always understood that I was going to be . . . y'know, I was listening to bass sounds on records and things like that. I was into that at a very early age."

(A nice story, but probably somewhat apocryphal—back in the mid-Fifties nobody was using the word "producer" in that sense. The producer was then the A & R man: Artist and Repertoire, or Artist and Recording man.)

It was inevitable that Spector would meet Leiber and Stoller. According to his own reports he had already met up with them in LA, where he was. Soon he was hanging out at the studio, even playing guitar on a few sessions.

Spector was on the move. His next step was characteristically bold. Unlike New York street groups who hung around the corners wailing their heads off just waiting for somebody to pick up on them, Phil took matters into his own hands. He had picked up an idea for a song one day when his mother took him to visit his father's grave in the Beth David cemetery at Elmont, Long Island. Inscribed on the tombstone stood the legend "To Know Him Was To Love Him." The Spector brain soon set to work. By mid-1958, he had created a song around that tag, changing the wording just a little. "I had an idea that it was a hit record."

The big step was to record it. He found a high school girl called Annette Kleinbard to sing the lead, went

45 RPM

(45-LB-5)

45 RPM

© 1958
Warman Music. Inc.
BMI 2:18

TO KNOW HIM, IS TO LOVE HIM
(Phillip Spector)

THE TEDDY BEARS

45-503

Spector's first hit record.

into a local studio, and overdubbed all the background harmonies himself. The group was called the Teddy Bears. The record cost him "about 40 dollars" to make. He managed to place it with a Los Angeles label called Dore.

By the end of 1958 "To Know Him Is To Love Him" had made number one in Billboard's chart, selling more than a million copies. It stayed on the chart for 23 straight weeks. The treatment of the song seemed so youthful and bitter-sweet, especially when the girl and boy sang the "and I do and I do and I do" echo bit, that it touched a million pubescent hearts. "To Know Him" was one of those records which surface every so often and touch the soft underbelly of pop; pure corn, they are nonetheless naive enough to be utterly convincing—anyone who isn't taken in by them must be a churl with a heart of stone.

"To Know Him" demonstrated in its structure that Spector had already mastered the kind of harmonic devices which then ruled pop. Most of the New York vocal group records, like the Five Satins' "In The Still of The Night," or the Penguins' "Earth Angel," were based on a cyclic progression: E-C sharp minor-B-A. It had an inevitability about it which let the listener know what was coming next and made him feel comfortable. Spector made one switch in the progression without losing any of the harmonic certainty, and wrote an eight-bar bridge whose declamatory appeal contrasted beautifully with the body of the song. Annette's confident little "oh-oh" at the end of the bridge after the words "that he was meant for me," is pure New York in content, just the kind of small improvisation which an East Coast singer would consider second nature, but the style is softer and whiter. In retrospect this record can be seen as the beginning of a Los Angeles style which later culminated in the Mama's and the Papa's, whose records were really little more than an updated Teddy Bears sound based on youthful, clean-cut, heavily arranged harmonies.

Lou Adler, who was to produce the Mama's and the Papa's almost a decade later, was already circulating in the LA music scene at the time of the Teddy Bears. Adler was organizing dances at roller rinks, at which the group appeared; he remembers them as "one of the first hit groups in LA, the sort of beginning of the West Coast music business." Adler first met Spector at the offices of Dore, where Adler was managing Jan and Dean. This famous duo's first hit, "Baby Talk," came out on Dore in the summer of '59, though of course later they went on to greater things with "Surf City," "The Little Old Lady From Pasadena," and others, all on Liberty. Most of Jan and Dean's best records were co-written by Brian Wilson, who, of all the later pop superstars, held Spector in the highest reverence.

The B side of "To Know Him" was perhaps even more interesting than the hit deck. "Don't You Worry My Little Pet" began with a guitar intro which might have come straight off an old Buddy Holly record—the whole side was far tougher and stronger. Here it is impossible to sort out a lead voice, because Phil, Annette, and the bass all weave in and out of each other, practically drowning the rudimentary backing. With the benefit of hindsight this curious mixture of folk and commercial R & B and heavy arrangement certainly seems a rehearsal for bigger things to come.

The follow-up to "To Know Him" was "Wonderful Lovable You," backed with "Till You're Mine," also on Dore. It didn't make the chart, but the Teddy Bears were signed by the larger Imperial label, also based in Los Angeles, who'd been notable for their hits wih Fats Domino, Ernie Freeman, Roy Brown, and others.

By this time, Spector and the group were on the road. Besides Phil and Annette, there was Marshall Leib, aged 19. Marshall was probably selected for the group as much for his beefcake appearance as for his voice. Imperial's publicity described him as "an all-round athlete . . . especially agile on the football field. He now attends Los Angeles City College where he majors in business law and music." Physically, Marshall was the absolute opposite of Phil: tall, dark, with the kind of profile which would set the female element of a Saturday night hop audience panting. Phil on the other hand appeared small and runty, with a pursed mouth and recessed chin. It sounds obvious, but the inadequacy of his stature contributed greatly to the birth and development of the success-devil inside him—like other small men he felt the need to prove himself, to show everyone that intellectual capacity could make brawn look stupid. Spector's slight stature was one of the roots of the paranoia which later pushed him to his greatest achievements.

While the Teddy Bears were on the road, an incident occurred which marked Phil's life for ever. Paul Case, later one of Spector's closest friends, tells it like this: "They were doing a one-nighter, and Phil went to the men's room. He went to the urinal, and four guys who'd come to see the show came in right after him and locked the door. They all urinated on him. I think this was the most shocking thing of his life." This indeed seems to have triggered Spector's obsession with his personal security, and has subsequently led him to surround himself at all times—even in the studio—with bodyguards. Case adds: "Sinatra was the same . . . the need to have something very physical surrounding him at all times. This incident, I think, was something that Phil never forgot, and he said to himself, 'This will never happen again.' It was quite an experience."

Besides the gymnasium hops and roller rink dances, the Teddy Bears also appeared on the important television shows: the Ed Sullivan Show, and Dick Clark's American Bandstand. Back then, the Clark show was particularly vital to the success of any rock and roll performer. The show itself had begun almost by accident when a crowd of teenagers wandered into the WFIL-TV studios in Philadelphia, on lunch break from school. They had heard the music playing from outside and had come in to investigate—and they stayed to dance. When the cameramen turned the lenses on them, a whole style of pop television was born, a style which, in the absence of any superior innovations, still has a stranglehold today. That first "accidental" show was such a success that the program instantly adopted the new format as standard. Before long it was being networked coast-to-coast. For teenagers all across America it became a focal point, a market-place they could watch every week to spot the latest styles in music, dancing, and clothes. At its peak, American Bandstand reached 40 million viewers. It got there first, and its power was astonishing. The program virtually created by itself the whole Philadelphia Sound of the late Fifties: Fabian Forte, for instance, lived in Philadelphia and, like most of the rest of the show's "talent," was used simply because he was readily available and fit the bill. He couldn't sing, but he could make the girls scream without even flickering an eyelash.

For singers, lip-synching became a new art to be mastered. Clark's men would play the hit record, and all the singer had to do was mime his way through it. "If the record was skipped it was really embarrassing," Phil remembers. However, "Dick Clark was the King; you just had to lip-synch his show and it was all right . . . things were a lot easier then."(1)

The Teddy Bears made at least three singles for Imperial, but only "Oh Why" made the chart, with "I Don't Need You Any More" on the B side. It entered the chart on March 15, 1959, reached number 91 the following week, and then disappeared. "Oh Why" isn't a very good record actually, and the people who bought it probably did so simply on the strength of the first hit. Annette puts a little more of herself into it, but the tune isn't nearly so memorable, while the whole effect drips saccharine. Virtually the only matter of interest is the production, which alters Annette's voice from sweet intimacy on the verse to a detached, angelic effect achieved by echo on the bridge. The B side, "I Don't Need You Any More," was merely pleasant rather than distinguished.

It was followed by two more singles—"If You Only

The first of three unsuccessful records for Imperial.

Knew (The Love I Have For You)" backed with "You Said Goodbye," and "Don't Go Away," backed with "Seven Lonely Days," neither of which made any showing on the charts. "Don't Go Away" was rather an attractive tune, but the arrangements were becoming stylized: Annette's voice now sounded more than a little ordinary, and Phil's dweezlings in the background almost reached the realm of self-parody. The piano and guitar arpeggios seemed trite instead of fresh and commanding. The whole formula was pretty much exhausted.

All these Imperial cuts, with the exception of "If You Only Knew," were included on the album called *The Teddy Bears Sing*. Looking at it now, the cover seems pure

kitsch. Phil and Marshall are wearing roll-and-veenecked
pastel blue college sweaters with "Teddy Bears" embroi-
dered in maroon across the chest and "Marshall" and "Phil"
high on the left breast. The picture was posed so long
ago that their trousers, with cuffs, are back in high fashion
as this is written—though not their white laced shoes, nor
their identical hairstyles, slicked back with greasy kid stuff,
pompadour in front, and the merest hint of pointy
sideburns. In the picture they are offering contrasting
blonde and brown teddy-bears to Annette, who displays
suitable signs of surprise and pleasure, but who really
doesn't look much better. Her bell-shaped skirt and white
stilettos tell the story. The whole presentation is about as
original as the album's title—no marks to Imperial's art
department.

The liner notes are equal fun. Of Annette Kleinbard,
who by this time had shortened her surname to the presumably more appealing Bard, they say: "Annette, the sixteen-
year-old lead voice of the trio, is a straight 'A' student
and had her mind set on psychology as a profession before
'To Know Him' hit." Phil's biggest problem, the notes
reveal, is "not to forget the tunes that keep running through
his mind. He never steps out of the house without a pencil
and notebook. It is not uncommon for him to interrupt
a date, dart out of a movie, or wake up in the middle
of the night to jot down a new song that pops into his
head."

There's also a rather ironic tribute to the supposed
power of teenagers in the music business: "The Teddy
Bears are a good example of how today's teenagers have
a chance to become famous in the record field. . . . In no
other field of creative or industrial endeavor can the
youngster express himself for so many and reap the lucrative rewards." (Tell that to Frankie Lymon, who died a

The Teddy Bears album; left to right: Marshall Leib, Annette Kleinbard, Phil Spector.

penniless junkie in 1968, just 12 years after his voice had been heard around the world.) The phrase about "reaping the lucrative rewards" takes on a particularly ironic note in the case of the Teddy Bears. In 1964 chronicler Tom Wolfe remarked of "To Know Him Is To Love Him" that "Spector made 20,000 dollars on that record, but somebody ran off with 17,000 dollars of it, and, well, no use going into that." (2) Spector made another salutary lesson out of the experience that would affect his business dealings for the rest of his career. In later years, John Lennon would comment: "Phil? Ha! He even charges you for breakfast."

But those same liner notes contained a paragraph which did lay down a real truth: "The Teddy Bears' success could not have happened ten years ago. Then, it was the name artists who turned out hit after hit. Record company brass were not as accessible to new talent as they are today. Buyers bought the artist rather than the rendition. Today, the newcomer has a better chance of scoring with a hit record than the name singer. People buy the sound, the arrangement, the beat, and the rhythm, and then look to see who the singers are."

Most of that could have been written by Spector himself as a kind of credo. Because of his belief in those words, he succeeded in the Sixties. Time and again, he was to prove that listeners didn't care whose name was on the label as long as the sound got through to them.

Apart from its four Spector compositions from various singles, his Teddy Bears album consisted of standards like "My Foolish Heart," "Long Ago And Far Away," "True Love," and "Tammy," a number one hit for Debbie Reynolds 18 months before. The best tracks were "Long Ago," written by Jerome Kern and George Gershwin, and the ever popular "Unchained Melody." The former is notable for the staccato, popping "bom-bom-bom" in the background by Phil, which effectively draws all attention away from Annette's very straight lead. Each ascending "bom" appears to be dubbed on separately, laying itself on top of its immediate predecessor and thus creating a pyramid effect. "Unchained Melody," one of those songs which steers carefully just to this side of schlock, is in fact inherently beautiful. It is further interesting because it acts as a preface to Phil's great classic version of the tune with the Righteous Brothers six years later. Here he contents himself with organizing the arpeggios beautifully, although the male harmonies in the intro and the ending definitely prefigure the Lettermen's biggest hit, "When I Fall In Love,"on Capitol in 1961.

Annette soon left the group to be replaced by a girl named Carol Connors. But the group was falling apart. Lou Adler remembers booking them for a roller-rink dance: "They came late and I had a fist fight with them. Phil showed up an hour late . . . he was really obnoxious at that time." With the verdict that "it was fun," Phil broke up the group. Marshall wasn't heard from again, although according to Phil, "Annette tried for years to make it in the record industry after that. She was on every label. Nothing happened." (This Annette should not be confused with the now legendary Annette Funicello, heroine of countless beach party movies, voice of many hits on the Disneyland and Vista labels, and ideal woman image to every clean cut American college boy.

By the time of the group's break-up, Phil had met Lester Sill, then in partnership with Lee Hazlewood and producing Duane Eddy's hit records for the Philadelphia-based Jamie label. Spector hung out with them in Hollywood—he says he played on some of the Duane Eddy records. Eddy was then being backed by the Rebels, like Larry Knechtel on keyboards and saxophonist Jim Horn, who were session men for recording purposes only. Spector became involved "just to learn a little bit and see what was going on." Still it was Sill and Hazlewood who gave him his next opportunity to record.

The cause was a hit record called "Come Softly To Me" by the Fleetwoods on Liberty, a song which reached the number one spot in the Spring of '59 just as the Teddy Bears were grinding to a halt. The leader of the Fleetwoods, a boy named Gary Troxel (the rest of the group consisted of two girls, Barbara and Gretchen), had obviously listened hard to what Spector had been doing with Annette.

"Come Softly To Me" refined the Teddy Bears' formula. Troxel began the record by singing alone in a candyfloss tenor: "Um dooby-doo dom dom dom dom-uh-doo-dom a-ooby-doo dom dom dom-uh-doo dom dom. . . ." This simple, catchy riff, was then joined by the two girls, who cooed, "Come softly, darling, come softly to me" while Gary continued to dooby-doo for all he was worth. The instrumental backing was restricted to gut-string guitar, double bass, and a vague tapping sound somewhere at the back of the mix. The tune was appealing, and the treatment was simple and repetitive—enough for it to click in a very big way.

Not exactly short on business acumen, Sill and Hazlewood thought it would be a good idea for Phil to cash in by making a record exactly in the Fleetwoods' style. How ironic, in view of the fact that "Come Softly To Me" was little more than a simple development of "To Know Him Is To Love Him!"

Phil did as suggested. He wrote a straight copy of "Come Softly To Me" called "I Really Do." The basic vocal riff had been inverted, while the tune, such as it was, sounded evey bit as ingenuous as that of its inspiration. The words would not set any cerebrums abulging either: "I want you/I need you/I really do" was exactly what was needed for such a record. Spector "just found some girl" to sing it, overdubbed all the male voice parts himself, and added only the rustling of wire brushes on a snare-drum under the intro. The product, however, put out under the name of The Spectors Three, was obviously a little too close to the Fleetwoods to catch the public's fancy, and it made no impression. The B side, "I Know

Why," was marginally tougher (the drummer actually used sticks), with Phil's double-tracked vocal set against a "heavenly" soprano wail from the girl. The best that can be said of it is that it was a true product of its era.

The record was released on Trey, a Hazlewood-Sill label distributed by Atlantic. The Spectors Three subsequently cut one more record, "My Heart Stood Still," backed with "Mr. Robin." That was a flop, too. It marked the end of Spector's career as a singer (although rumor has it that he cut a vocal side under the name Phil Harvey, titled "Willie Boy," for the Emerald label). So far Phil had not proven himself a heavy talent. But he was only 18, and he'd been learning. . . .

One of Spector's more obscure ventures.

4

ON BROADWAY
"All those records,
it's so hard to remember...."

THERE ARE TWO VERSIONS OF THE STORY OF how Phil Spector arrived in New York.

The first, and most appealing in terms of Spector's image, has been widely disseminated by Tom Wolfe in his essay "The First Tycoon of Teen," and is endorsed by the tycoon himself. The second, and more prosaic, is based on the reminiscences of Mike Stoller.

Both stories agree that Spector, after his stints with the Teddy Bears and the Spectors Three, took training to become a court stenographer. Imagine Spector, his head bursting with noise, sitting in a dusty courtroom on a summer afternoon, flies buzzing around the jury's heads, taking down every word of the hearing on a silent, high-speed typewriter. More than a little incongruous, I'm sure you'll agree—but certified fact, nonetheless.

Wolfe's version has it that Spector planned to study at UCLA, but couldn't whip up the necessary money because of the monetary hassles over "To Know Him Is To Love Him." Court reporting was the alternative.

But Spector wanted to go to New York. As his mother had taught him to speak and write passable French, it was decided that he become an interpreter at the United Nations headquarters, where both his linguistic and steno-graphic ability would provide the necessary qualifications.

A job was duly obtained, and Spector took off from the Los Angeles airport on a plane bound for New York. With nowhere to stay on arrival, he looked up Leiber and Stoller and slept the night in their office. The next morning he simply did not go to the UN. He never went, in fact. Instead he stayed on with Leiber and Stoller and became entrenched in the music business.

Wolfe's story depends in part on Spector's previous acquaintance with Leiber and Stoller, to which Spector himself attests. Speaking of the period before the Teddy Bears, Spector says: "I'd met Jerry and Mike . . . before, and I'd played on some things." Of the night he arrived in New York, he told me that he met "Jerry and Mike. I slept on their office desk. It's a silly story, but it's true."

Stoller contradicts much of Wolfe's version. He maintains that he didn't know Spector at all on the West Coast—that the first he heard of him was when Lester Sill called from Los Angeles to say "he had this bright, talented fellow who was interested in producing, and who didn't want to stay in California.

"We said send him in," Stoller continues. "We sent him his fare, as I recall, and he stayed at Jerry's home for a while. We signed him as a writer and producer, and he started coming to our sessions."

The discrepancy between stories is not surprising. This period of Spector's life, from late '59 through mid '62, is riddled with unknowns. Because he wasn't important then, most of the people around him do not recall his exact function at any given time. Spector himself has either forgotten or prefers not to remember. When questioned on specifics he's inclined to say: "I don't even remember those days. . . . If you show me pictures of myself, I don't even know who I am. I don't know what I was doing there or how I fit in. I could never identify with myself."

Tracking down just what he did do, then, is no easy task. But some things are certain. It is obvious that this was the formative period of his musical life, when he picked up the knowledge and "feelings" for the expression of emotion through musical technique, knowledge which has informed his work ever since.

It is further a fact that he was apprenticed to Leiber and Stoller, at their offices in the Brill Building, 1619 Broadway, for some months. He told me: "It's funny . . . you think back about everybody that was making hits . . . 'Lavender Blue,' I was making all those records, but I wasn't getting any credit. I was writing songs for Elvis Presley, and I wasn't getting any credit, but I didn't care, because the people in the business were finding out, and that's what was important—getting a reputation."

"Lavender Blue," Sammy Turner's big hit, reached number three in mid-1959—the date makes it unlikely that Spector was involved in its production. Stoller—who, with his partner, has always been given credit for the record's production—denies that Spector had any part in it. Still, Spector's story is possible. Leiber and Stoller certainly did allow their apprentices to produce records under the overall company name with no individual credit. To confuse matters more, in the finale of "Lavender Blue," Turner lets rip with a wail of pure Righteous Brothers, whom Phil was to mold in later years.

Spector certainly attended the famous sessions which Leiber and Stoller produced for the Drifters, probably beginning with the "Save The Last Dance For Me" session in May, 1960—from which session three other cuts—"Nobody But Me," "I Count The Tears," and "Sometimes I Wonder"—also emerged. But he may also have been present at the August '59 session for "True Love, True Love" and "Dance With Me," and at the December '59 session for "This Magic Moment" and "Lonely Wind."

On some if not all of these, he was contracted to play rhythm guitar. He must have been strongly impressed and influenced by what was going on, in particular by Stoller's arrangements, which used strings and Latin percussion in subtle abundance. The Latin Tinge helped shape his rhythmic outlook most of all. Stoller had introduced it in March '59 on a Drifters record called "There Goes My Baby"—now generally credited with being the first R&B record to employ strings. The session which produced that record was perhaps one of the most extraordinary sessions since the invention of the phonograph and is well documented in Bill Millar's book, *The Drifters*(1). At least as important in the long run as the bizarre, fascinating string arrangement on the recording was the innovatory use of a Latin-American rhythm, the Baion. Until that time, the Baion had not been used at all in blues or rock, though now you hear it everywhere. It certainly served the Drifters well, as the basis of "Save The Last Dance," "This Magic Moment," and "When My Little Girl Is Smiling," among others.

The Baion's "bom bom-bom" riff has permeated pop music. It was a strong factor in the rhythmic side of the Mersey Boom groups, four and five years later—Lennon, McCartney, and all the rest had certainly listened to their Drifters records. Spector, who was right in there all the time, could not avoid picking it up on many of his later records. The use of the strings here also had its great importance. In "Save The Last Dance," for instance, they were used sparingly in the first half of the song, playing a thin, ethereal harmonic strand above the vocal. In the brief instrumental bridge, they swept into prominence, with violins on an irresistible line while cellos provided a throaty variation, as much for rhythmic punctuation as for melodic contrast. Notably, the string players used a strong attack quite unlike the watery sound we came to expect from violins in pop music; they had all the fire of a good sax section, but a sweeter, more romantic style. In the wide space between percussion and strings, swaying acoustic guitars played a complementary rhythmic pattern to which they adhered strictly throughout the record.

Spector remembered all these ideas and later exploited them: he built his greatest records around a guitar base, with strings playing those high, wild harmonics only just within reach of the human ear. Spector also followed Leiber and Stoller's lead in distinctly subordinating the back-up vocal group to the lead. A back-up group became just that—they did not improvise at all, but served and sounded as a buttress to the lead melody. In all these ways, Jerry Leiber, and particularly Mike Stoller, had an absolutely vital influence on Spector.

The lead singer on those Drifters records was Ben E. King, formerly of a group called the Crowns. The Crowns became the Drifters when manager George Treadwell sacked the original group but was forced to find replacements to fill a ten-year contract at the Apollo. Although King sang lead on no more than 11 Drifters sides, he is by far their best remembered leader, thanks to "There Goes My Baby," "Dance With Me," and "Save The Last Dance," the latter of which became the group's only number one record late in 1960.

King was one of the finest singers ever to grace popular music. His baritone was full and rich but never plummy, his phrasing was lean and surprisingly sinuous, and he would draw out across the beat a line of ecstatic hums and moans in a beautiful tension building way. He sounded like no one else—even the most cloth-eared kid could recognize him 50 paces away from a transistor.

Ironically enough, he left the Drifters shortly before "Save The Last Dance" was released—a dispute with Treadwell may have been the cause. But everybody knew who sang lead on that record. King's was a hot name.

Around the time of "Save The Last Dance," Spector and Leiber wrote a song for King called "Spanish Harlem." They cut it with an arrangement by Mike Stoller (probably roughed out by Stoller and filled in by Stan Appelbaum), and on the same session—Spector remembers it was a standard three-hour date—they also made "Stand By Me," "First Taste of Love," and one other. "First Taste" was also written by Spector, this time with lyrics by Doc Pomus, one of the best lyricists of our time. (In partnership with Mort Shuman, Pomus wrote an apparently endless string of songs which consistently tapped a rich vein of emotion: "Lonely Avenue" for Ray Charles, "His Latest Flame" and "Little Sister" for Elvis Presley, "Save The Last Dance For Me" and "I Count The Tears" for the Drifters, "Here Comes The Night" for Ben E. King . . . you could go on forever.)

"Spanish Harlem" was an unbeatable record. Leiber's lyrics were so evocative of their area and told such a lovely story (not many people could get the words "rose" and "concrete" in the same verse and make it sound so *right*), and Spector's tune was so simple, just the right suggestion of Flamenco plus an unexpected tightening up in the middle lines of each verse, that the song truly echoes one of Leiber's phrases: ". . . soft and sweet and dreaming." Stoller's arrangement is as spare as can be—just bass and bass drum playing the Baion rhythm in soft unison, with a choked triangle playing a constant, almost subliminal, eight-to-the-bar. A dry, evocative marimba answers King's phrases; when the strings sweep in, they play off an eloquent soprano saxophonist who ends his solo with a tumbling sketch of Spain. The entire song demands quoting:

There is a rose in Spanish Harlem
A rare rose up in Spanish Harlem
It is a special one
It's never seen the sun
It only comes out when the moon is on the run
And all the stars are gleaming
It's growing in the street
Right up through the concrete
But soft and sweet and dreaming
There is a rose in Spanish Harlem
A rare rose up in Spanish Harlem
With eyes as black as coal
That look down in my soul
And start a fire there and then I lose control
I have to beg your pardon
I'm going to pick that rose
And watch her as she grows
In my garden

©1960 Progressive Music Publishing Co., Inc., and Trio Music. Used by permission.

BEN E. KING

THE DRIFTERS LONDON RECORDS

48 West 48th Street
New York, N.Y.

The Drifters at the time when Ben E. King (second from left) was lead singer.

Ben E. King

I suppose it's about as perfect as a pop record can ever be. In the second month of 1961 it reached number ten on the Billboard chart, with the flip, "First Taste Of Love," hitting number 53 in its own right. That was a good song too, though not quite so special: the high point comes when Bennie goes "mmmmm" just between the first and second verses.

"Stand By Me," written by Bennie himself with Leiber and Stoller (under their collective *nom de plume* of "Elmo Glick"), was King's next single. When his third single, "Here Comes The Night," didn't do well, the record was flipped over, and a song called "Young Boy Blues," once again by Spector and Pomus, started getting the plays. This flip side is an okay but unspectacular blues-ballad. By comparison with this Spector-Pomus cut, "Here Comes The Night" is a magnificently risky record, all dancing guitars and subtle rhythms.

One thing which makes these Baion-style records unique is the frequent total absence of conventional drums—a quite revolutionary move. The Baion required something more graceful than previous R & B rhythms. Stoller depended on a combination of triangle or shakers, bass drum or muffled tom-tom, playing in unison with string bass or bass guitar.

It made a considerable mark on the young Spector. "If you listen to a lot of those records," he says, "there's no real drum on any of them. They're like tom-toms, beating . . . it was strange, a lot of those records are strange. We just used 'bom bom-bom' and let it carry the record along." At this time virtually everything was being recorded "live" with no overdubs.

Spector was meeting a lot of important people now, people like Ahmet Ertegun and Jerry Wexler of Atlantic Records, and Paul Case, a figure almost unknown outside the music business but a vitally important influence on the pop scene in those days. Case was General Professional Manager of Hill and Range Music, a publishing house owned by the Aberbach family. Hill and Range owned many important songs and writers, including much of Elvis Presley's recorded repertoire.

Case was later primarily responsible for starting the career of Burt Bacharach. Case guided Bacharach towards the Drifters, where the song writer made his first big hit with "(Don't Go) Please Stay" (Atlantic 2105). Case also helped Bert Berns, who later produced the Drifters, Solomon Burke, the McCoys, and Van Morrison, and owned the Bang and Shout labels.

In addition, Case was the first person to use a song by a young writer called Barry Mann. Mann's "Stranded" appeared on the B side of Bobby Pedrick's "White Bucks And Saddle Shoes" on the Big Top label in 1958. (Big

Top was affiliated with Hill and Range.) Three years later, Barry Mann had a hit novelty song called "Who Put The Bomp" (ABC 10237) and also married another writer named Cynthia Weil. Together they were destined to assist Spector on some of the best records he ever made. Around 1960, Hill and Range was doing a lot of business with Leiber and Stoller, partly because the latter were writing prolifically for Presley. Lester Sill brought Spector to meet Case, who remembers Phil first as a writer.

"When he first came in," Case says, "he was writing with a girl called Beverley Ross. He collaborated with her for about six months. . . . I don't think anything important came of it, although I think they wrote some pretty good songs. Phil was looking for *the* writer, for someone to work with, and he was trying out a few people."

Shortly after meeting Case, Leiber and Stoller recommended Spector to Big Top as a producer, and he was put in charge of a session for Ray Peterson, a talented white soft-pop singer whose biggest hit had been the Jeff Barry-written "Tell Laura I Love Her" on RCA, the unforgettable death song. The session was for the Dunes label, a company owned by Stan Schulman and distributed by Big Top.

Phil produced Peterson on an updated version of the old Folk/Blues standard "Corinna Corinna." It was a pleasant record, with effectively light electric guitar. A strong selling point was the way Spector matched Peterson's voice with that of a sweet soprano on the opening line of the chorus. A very professionally made commercial record, it went to number nine around Christmas, 1960. It was Phil Spector's first hit in New York. To cap it all, he'd co-written the B side, "Be My Girl."

Peterson's follow-up, "Sweet Little Kathy" (Dunes 2004), is such a blatant pinch from the treatment of

"Corinna" that one cannot believe Spector produced it. Peterson doesn't sing well on the record, which strengthens the belief that Spector had nothing to do with it, because through working with King and the Drifters he now knew what a good singer was. And ever since then he's spent much of his career extracting wondrous performances from singers of sometimes minimal talent.

No, Spector's next record for Dunes was Curtis Lee's "Pretty Little Angel Eyes." Lee was a singer in the Fabian mold, which is to say that he wasn't really a singer at all, but just a very good-looking boy who got the girls hot. Spector made him sound good, though. "Angel Eyes" is a fine rocker in the Dion and the Belmonts vein, with weaving harmony and a very solid rhythm section. It made an average song, written by Lee and Tommy Boyce (later half of a successful duo with Bobby Hart, on A & M), into

Among Spector's first independent productions were records by Ray Peterson and Curtis Lee.

something quite good enough to make the Top Ten late in '61.

The follow-up, three months later, was another Lee-Boyce epic, this time called "Under The Moon Of Love," and is almost as good—raunchier, somewhat in the wild U.S. Bonds vein, but toned down a little for general consumption. The B side was sheer teen genius: Boyce deserves a medal for starting a lyric with the immortal words "Beverly Jean, she is my teenage queen." Spector provided great backing with rolling tom-tom interludes, and the rough tenor sax occasionally bursting through.

The Curtis Lee records indicate another strong influence on Spector: the New York male vocal groups which sprang up in Black, Puerto Rican, and Italian areas of the city. These groups mostly took the form of street corner quartets harmonizing *a cappella*, creating a true and entirely unselfconscious form of folk music which most people today call "Doo-wop," since it sounds like the noise that the bass singers used to make.

Spector called the records such groups made "those awful good records—'Little Star,' by the Elegants, or 'Angel Baby' by Rosie and the Originals.' Those are awful, awful records that I love. You love those records because you know they're honest, and that's it." Among his favorites were the Dovells (with Len Barry), Dion and the Belmonts, and the Crests. "Dion wasn't imitating anybody in the way he sang," he says. "He sang like a New York kid on a street corner. The old groups in the old days, you'd be sitting around and that bass riff would go 'doop doop' and that'd be a smash, right there you knew you had it." (2) That, he felt, was an honest way to make music—and hit records. Like the Sun records—he had a real affection for that kind of music, and he understood how to integrate it into his own concept.

Phil at this time was also becoming a little . . . unusual. He'd always been very bright, a real autodidact who listened to classical music when he wasn't digging the Elegants, and who walked around with a book on French history under his arm.

But the first real sign that he was quite different from the hundred and one junior producers then dashing around New York came when he started to grow his hair around 1961. Two, three years before the Beatles Phil was growing his locks in curls down his neck and onto his shoulders. He was persecuted for it of course. People would shout "Hey, there's Shirley Temple" after him in the street. When he began to affect a big black cloak he earned the sobriquet "D'Artagnan," which stuck among his intimates for a good number of years. Everybody who knew him in those days still gives a wry shrug and says something like: "I'd never seen anything like it." And can you imagine the looks he got from the session men, not to mention the Broadway bar flies?

It was certainly a good way to get noticed—his name was getting around to the right places. When he arrived in New York no one had known quite what to expect, although they knew of his involvement with the Teddy Bears. Paul Case sums it up: "He didn't have that much of a background, just a great potential, which everybody suspected. They suspected that, because Leiber and Stoller—who had a good feeling for talent—worked with him right away. Yeah . . . you suspected, you felt it . . . you had an instinct for something, and you had an instinct for Phil Spector."

But for some people he was a little hard to take. Tony Orlando, a young New York singer who was making hit songs by Carole King and Gerry Goffin ("Bless You" and "Halfway to Paradise," both on Epic, were the biggest), remembers seeing Phil walk into a BMI dinner in, he thinks,

1961: "His hair was shoulder length, in what we call a page-boy, flipped up *this* way, both sides and the back . . . and when a guy walked into a room with long hair in '61, he was really a freak. You think there are freaks walking around now? Well, that was *really* being freaky, really being anti-Establishment."

By this time Phil had severed his connections with Leiber and Stoller. "He broke the contract with us, because he said he was under age when he signed it," says Stoller. "I don't think we were thrilled about it at the time, but people have to go the way they're happy."

He went to work at Atlantic as an A & R man. At that time he was very close to Ahmet Ertegun, of whom he constantly performed a startlingly accurate impersonation. He was there for a few months, but nothing of note came out of it. Spector himself has mentioned producing "You Must Have Been A Beautiful Baby" for Bobby Darin, on the Atlantic subsidiary label Atco, and it's quite likely. (I would guess that he may have also produced Darin's unusually atmospheric version of the standard "Nature Boy," mainly because the tympani-style percussion has "Spector '61" stamped all over it.)

But that seems to have been the sum total of his output for Atlantic. It is possible that he quit because the label concentrated more on Blues-oriented sounds than on what he wanted at the time.

So he left to become a freelance producer, making hits for anyone and everyone who asked. "I made a lot of records that were hits that I didn't put my name on, because I couldn't," he says. "I took my three hundred dollars and ate for a month and some other guy got the producer credit. And I didn't care, because I knew the people in the business would find out, and that was all I really cared about." (3)

We'll probably never know exactly how many

records he did produce at that time, but the ones which are known for sure make a pretty mixed bunch.

There's one with Gene Pitney, for instance. A young singer, writer, and, like Spector, a multi-instrumentalist (guitar, piano, and drums), Pitney had already had his first hit—his own song "(I Wanna) Love My Life Away" on the Musicor label—by the time he came into contact with Spector. For Pitney's next record, Spector went to his favorite source of material: Aldon Music, owned by Donny Kirshner and Al Nevins. There Phil found a Carole King/Gerry Goffin composition called "Every Breath I Take," a perfect Drifters-style song. It was only natural—the same writers had come up with "When My Little Girl Is Smiling" and "Some Kind Of Wonderful" for the Drifters.

Spector produced a recording worthy of his mentors, Leiber and Stoller. Based on a liberal use of pedal-tympani as rhythmic and harmonic punctuation, it gives the track a very heavy sound, which is opposed by the formula string writing. The drummer plays a strong role, surging through the breaks with jerky, emotional snare-drum fills, while background voices are exceptionally well integrated with the arrangement. Pitney sings imaginatively, making effective use of a strangulated falsetto, and steering clear of the whining tone which characterized his biggest records later on.

Spector produced one other track with Pitney, a song called "Dream For Sale" which he had co-written with Terry Phillips, another of his early collaborators. Both these tracks, along with the rest of Pitney's early singles, can be found on an album called *The Many Sides of Gene Pitney* (Musicor MU 2001). The Spector-produced cuts have a noticeably bigger sound than the others, on which production is credited to Pitney's manager, Aaron Schroeder.

Next came a commission from his old friends Lester Sill and Lee Hazlewood: a couple of records with a trio called the Paris Sisters, for their new Gregmark label, named after their publishing company. Phil returned briefly to the West Coast to make the records. They first cut a song by Barry Mann and Larry Kolber called "I Love How You Love Me." That, says Spector, was "just a remake of 'To Know Him Is To Love Him,' it's the same sound and everything."

True enough. Slow, mushy, based on those oh-so-delicate arpeggios again, it captured the same sort of romantic following. Who could fail to be ensnared by the purity of the lead Sister's voice? Spector had arranged it with a care for musical economy; the single string line, rising and falling like a heaving breast, imparts that essential feeling of "sweet sorrow." In retrospect, this might also be one of the producer's most important pre-Philles records. Listen to the distant quality of the strings—in that line of overtones without the basic note, it's possible to hear everything that Spector ever did with strings in later years.

It was a natural Top Ten hit, which came soon after the Pitney record. Spector also cut the follow-up, a King Goffin number called "He Knows I Love Him Too Much." Again very attractive, but it was not nearly as memorable, although I'm very fond of the clever two guitar arrangement, and the strings are slightly fuller.

Spector was now writing regularly with Hank Hunter, a freelancer who later became a staff writer for Screen Gems. Together they penned a song called "Second-Hand Love," which Paul Case thought good for Connie Francis, who already had three Number Ones and ten other Top Ten records. So Case took Spector to the Copacabana in New York where Connie was working, and introduced them.

The meeting was fruitful. Phil produced the song with Connie for MGM. It's difficult to say how it would have sounded with any other singer, but it certainly appears tailor-made for Miss Francis, very much in the Country-style weeping ballad bag of hers. It may be my imagination, but I find it marginally less offensive than most of her other big ones. She isn't allowed to over-emote, as was her usual wont. Beyond that, there's not much to say about it. It was just another hit record, something else to throw in people's faces to show them that Philip Spector was a natural-born hitmaker with the golden touch, whatever the musical style. It gave Connie her eleventh Top Ten side.

Before this, though, Spector had come to the attention of Snuffy Garrett, ace production head of Liberty Records (responsible for the best Bobby Vee hits, and countless others). Garrett offered him a job, probably similar to his A & R post at Atlantic.

Yet again nothing came of the liaison. Paul Case has just one vivid memory of Spector's sojourn at Liberty: "He had this tremendous office. He had a big desk about ten feet along, and to see Phil behind this big desk. . . . He used to fool around with a hockey game, one of those games you can shoot, and the only recollections we ever had of going up to the office were of him, the desk, and the game. He started on a few projects, but I don't think anything important happened there."

It is certain that, between 1960 and 1962, Spector made many other records, most of which we'll probably never learn about. He calls them "those *silly* records," and in at least one case he's right. That is a single by Ray Sharpe (who recorded previously for the Trey and Jamie labels), cut for the Garex label in the early Sixties. It was a song called "Hey Little Girl," and it really was one of the silliest things I've ever heard, a novelty tune with a skiffle feeling which never made any impact. The only surprise is that it took two such heavy talents as Spector and Richie Barrett (former lead singer with the Valentines as well as Goldner's talent scout) to write it. As far as I know, it was the only time they ever collaborated.

It is also said that Spector produced a record called "Some of Your Loving" with Johnny Nash, the R & B singer who brought out hits for ABC between '57 and '59.

All the records discussed in this chapter were produced to impress the people in the business, to get Spector's name around, to show them just what a flexible producer he was. After hits with the Paris Sisters, Ben E. King, and Connie Francis, it must have looked as though he could take any kind of virgin clay and mold it into a smash.

But already, well before the end of this freelance period, moves were under way which were finally to set him on the true path of his ultimate goal: unfettered creation of those crazy sounds whirling round his head.

5

LITTLE SYMPHONIES FOR THE KIDS
"They all said it couldn't be done...."

SOMETIME DURING THE MIDDLE OF 1961, PAUL Case introduced Spector to Helen Noga, who was then managing Johnny Mathis. "She was looking to expand," Case remembers. "She wanted to go into production, into financing and publishing, in addition to what she had."

Spector, too, was looking for something: money, to finance the making of records with a group he'd found in New York called the Crystals. He didn't want to place them with a major label—the time had come at last to go out on his own, he figured, to begin the realization of his dream.

An arrangement was agreed upon: Noga would finance, Spector would produce, and Lester Sill would take care of business. It was a good set-up that covered all possible angles, and Phil, feeling that he couldn't serve two gods, left Liberty.

They named the label Philles, after Phil and Les(ter). Phil began work with the Crystals on the record which was to become Philles 100. In the beginning, the Crystals consisted of Barbara, Pat, and Dee Dee—all 17 years old—and Mary and Lala, both 16. None of them was exactly beautiful; they looked rather gauche and ingenuous, the kind of girls who, posing for their first album cover, wore wrist-length white gloves which matched their shoes. They were like the girl next door, in mildly flouncy pastel-and-lace dresses and respectable, processed hairstyles.

But in the beginning the image didn't matter, because they were not being seen. It was the sound that counted, and the Crystals were what Spector needed—a fair copy of the Shirelles, the group who initiated the New York Girl Group sound back in '60 with the classic King/Goffin song "Will You Love Me Tomorrow" on Scepter.

The NYGG sound depended first on the seductive tone of the girls' voices. Shirley Owens of the Shirelles sang in an urgent, come-hither voice which, while not particularly "musical" in terms of control and technique, nevertheless presented a fascinating blend of knowingness and innocence. The subject matter of NYGG songs displayed a similar ambivalence. The boys celebrated by the Shirelles often were regarded by the community as "bad boys," though they really had hearts of pure gold. If only the girls could reach out far enough and penetrate that tough exterior, they would find a sweet man to take care of them for the rest of their lives.

The Shirelles had the sound down pat. Later on the Chiffons would bring it to an absolute peak with "He's So Fine." And right now the Crystals had it too.

The first record was cut at Mirasound Studios, at 145 West 47th Street in New York, on a three-track machine with Bill MacMeekan at the controls. Phil had picked two songs that he had co-written: "There's No Other (Like My Baby)," composed in collaboration with one L. Bates, about whom posterity is silent, and "Oh Yeah, Maybe Baby," written with Hank Hunter. These two cuts formed the first release. Also on the label appeared the name of Mother Bertha Music—the publishing company Spector had just formed. It was named for his mother.

"There's No Other" was a particularly fine song, solidly based on the E-C sharp minor-A-B progression, with a completely unforgettable chorus and a seamless verse. Young Barbara Alston took the lead here, and sung her heart out, particularly on the lovely, suspenseful, *rubato* intro. It was quite a big record, too: listen to the cooing of the other girls behind Barbara on the verse, then think of what the Ronettes would be doing in a couple of years. Listen also to the production job on the drums: the way the cymbal swishes fluidly in 12/8 time, while the snare lets loose a hard, echoey back beat. There are strings on this cut, too—arranged by either Arnold Goland or Hank Levine (the latter noted for his hit with the instrumental "Image," on ABC at exactly this time)—but even when the strings aren't playing, the track sounds *full*—much more than just the piano, guitar, bass, and drums which are there.

Barbara also took the lead on "Oh Yeah, Maybe Baby"—an altogether lighter song based on the good old Baion, complete with tom-toms, clattering castanets, and choked triangle (no cymbal, snare, or bass drum). The whole cut is extremely Driftersish, particularly in the brief instrumental break, where the violins match the cellos in exactly the same manner as on "Save The Last Dance For Me" or "Here Comes The Night."

The record was released in October, 1961. "Oh Yeah" may have been intended as the original A side: in the blank space occupied by the run-off grooves of each Philles record, there was always a little code number in addition to the usual matrix number. A Ronettes' record, for instance, would bear the code "R-10" or "R-20," indicating that these would be the tenth or twentieth songs cut by the Ronettes. A Bob B. Soxx record would have a "BBS" code, plus a number—thus Soxx's first record "Zip-a-dee-doo-dah," is "BBS-1." The A side always had the lower number—"Oh Yeah, Maybe Baby" was "TCY-1," while "There's No Other" was "TCY-2." The TCY code stayed with the Crystals through all their Philles recordings.

Whichever was intended as A side, it was "There's No Other" which first showed in Billboard's Hot 100, on November 16. It stayed in the lists for 11 weeks, reaching number 20—very encouraging indeed.

The next Philles record, 101, initiated a series of three which had nothing to do with Spector: "Here I Stand" backed with "You're My Only Love," by somebody called Jolly Scott; 103, an instrumental coupling of "Chopsticks" and "Malaguena," by Ali Hassan; and 104, apparently never released, listed only in the Philles catalogue as "Lt. Col. Bogey's Parade" with no artist given.

Philles 102 was the Crystals' follow-up, called "Uptown." It could well have been the answer to "Spanish Harlem." Spector arranged it himself with a very pronounced Flamenco feel, accentuated with running single-string Spanish guitar and castanets.

The song was originally written by Barry Mann and his wife, Cynthia Weil, for Tony Orlando. But Phil said it was a girl's song, the story of a boy who, every morning, goes to work Downtown "where everyone's his boss." At night, though, it's a different story: he comes back home to his girl in the ghetto, and "the world is

The first single and the first album by the Crystals

sweet, it's at his feet ... when he's Uptown." It's a very touching story, travelling the edges of racial and social barriers. Violins complement the story with nervous plucked figures during the "Downtown" section before sweeping into whirling bowed phrases for the passage expressing happiness and security. It works perfectly.

The B side featured a quite ordinary ballad called "What A Nice Way To Turn Seventeen," written by Jack Keller and Larry Kolber who, as with the Mann/Weil and Goffin/King partnerships, were staff writers at Aldon Music.

"Uptown" was even more successful than the first record. Entering the chart in March of '62, it soon scooted up to number 13, and hung around the list for three months before quitting.

People were beginning to take notice of Phil and his label. It was obvious he had the ability to make hits, even if his hits sounded—as yet—like those of other people. Something was happening all right.

Around this time Phil hung out at Donny Kirshner's offices in the Brill Building a great deal—and he got the pick of Donny's writing talent: Barry and Cynthia, Carole and Gerry, and others. "Phil and Donny were funny to watch together," Tony Orlando remembers. "Phil used to say that the two people he'd most like to be like were Donny Kirshner and Gene Aberbach, of Hill and Range Music. Gene came to America from Austria, and he was very bright. He wanted to be American so bad that the first thing he did was learn baseball, and now he's an expert on it . . . there's nothing he doesn't know about it. He can also write songwriters' agreements in his sleep . . . he just knows his business, and Phil used to respect Gene very much.

"He liked Kirshner's creativity and his childlike, almost naive manner. To watch Spector and Kirshner together was to see two really egocentric people, with a great amount of drive and ambition. Phil knew there was some great material up there in Donny's office, because Carole was a great writer and Barry was a great writer. His relationship with Barry really grew quicker, but he started going up there because of Carole, I think. Of course, Donny was trying to make deals with him."

It was all going very smoothly. In July, 1962, Phil put out the third Crystals single—Philles 105. The topside was a Goffin/King song called "He Hit Me (And It Felt Like A Kiss)," with a Spector/Goffin/King collaboration, "No One Ever Tells You," on the flip.

The trade magazines picked it for a smash. *Cashbox* called it "a fabulous beat-ballad romancer . . . watch it zoom into top-tensville" while *Billboard* said: "Much thought went into the lyrics on these two unique sides. . . . ['He Hit Me'] is a serious ballad with a telling message while ['No One Ever Tells You'] notes the pain and complexity of life. Either or both could be winners."

They weren't. The radio started playing the A side, and suddenly people began to listen to the words. "He hit me? And it felt like a kiss? What're these people trying to *say,* fergodsake? That's sado-whatsit! I ain't having none of that Commie porn on *my* show!" Self-censorship and listeners' complaints were enough to cause "He Hit Me" to be abruptly withdrawn from the market, before it had time to do any real "harm."

The action of the boy in the song may not have been entirely laudable, but after all he only hit the girl because she'd been going out with someone else—and in the end they kissed and made up in perfect bliss. Harmless, but most people would only listen to the first two lines.

The arrangement may not have helped either. It was so simple as to be positively stark. The backing voices were somehow too shrill, and a double-time rhythm which entered half way through was curiously unsettling. It was a little unnerving, in an oddly intangible way.

But off the market it came, so instead Phil concentrated on putting out the first Crystals album, *Twist Uptown.* Created to cash in on the then current Twist craze, it included only one real Twist number, a very mediocre song called "Frankenstein Twist," written by two gentlemen called Henry and McCorkle.

The album included all the sides so far released on singles except "He Hit Me" (since the first side of the album has only five titles, it may have been pulled off at the last minute). There were in addition a Spector/Pomus song called "Another Country—Another World," a Spector/Hunter number titled "I Love You Eddie" (perhaps the most undistinguished song Phil ever wrote: the second

HE HIT ME
(And It Felt Like A Kiss)
(C. King-G. Geoffin)

Aldon Music, Inc.
BMI
P-TCY 5
Time: 2:28

THE CRYSTALS
Prod. PHIL SPECTOR
105

PHILLES RECORDS · 6816 SUNSET BLVD. · HOLLYWOOD 28, CALIFORNIA

PHILLES RECORDS

**The Crystals, left to right: Barbara Alston, Lala Brooks, Pat
Wright, and Dee Dee Kennibrew; and the ill-fated "He Hit Me,"
on which Barbara sang lead, with reviews from** *Billboard* **and**
Cashbox.

line is ". . . but so does Betty"); Carla Thomas's lovely hit tune "Gee Whiz" (here given a beautiful treatment with soft, pleading voices), and—believe it or not—yet another Goffin/King sado-masochistic classic, "Please Hurt Me." The story line of this one ran: "If you gotta hurt somebody, please hurt me." What *were* Carole and Gerry up to in the summer of '62? It is actually a pleasant song—the composers cut a rather better version of it the following year with their own protege, Little Eva, as B side of "Let's Start The Party Again," on Dimension.

There was finally, on *Twist Uptown*, a new Mann/Weil song called "On Broadway." With its castanet treatment, it evoked the lure of the bright lights almost as effectively as "Uptown"—with one major difference. Phil plugged a few holes in the latter part of the song by inviting Steve Douglas, his session saxophonist, to play a solo on soprano sax. Douglas comes up with the most extraordinary improvisations, limp and loose and just *weird*, like someone who couldn't play the horn properly. But when you're used to it, it becomes very effective.

Later on, in March 1963, Spector was to participate in a more famous recording of this song with the Drifters, Rudy Lewis singing lead. For this later session, the words were altered by Jerry Leiber, who was supervising the session with Mike Stoller. "On Broadway" became an absolutely perfect song, capturing exactly the atmosphere of that outlandish vortex where 52nd Street crosses Broadway, near the Colony record store and Lloyd Price's Turntable. The whole history of the American popular music business is crystallized in that corner, in the neon and the pimps and the hustlers and the whores, and the Drifters' version of the song reflects it perfectly.

Phil's participation in the session stands out more obviously than usual: he plays the extraordinary curling

guitar breaks between the violin and trumpet figures. Spector had played rhythm guitar on many of the group's
records. On this particular session, he remembers, "the
Drifter guitar player was ill or drunk or something. I don't
know what happened to him, but yeah, I played it. I'd
done the song before, with the Crystals, so I knew it very
well, and I knew what Jerry wanted." Those four bars
of very impressionistic guitar were extremely unusual for
their time.

Back at Philles though, a revolution was about to
take place. Phil wasn't entirely happy with his partners,
and realized that he could now do without them, thus
fulfilling his wish to be entirely self-sufficient. So he bought
out Sill and Helen Noga, and prepared to go it alone.
Since then he has referred to 1962 as the beginning of
Philles, as though the first year was really something else
altogether.

Spector also changed the whole set-up. Up until
that time, his records had been distributed and promoted
by two men, Harold Lipsius and Harry Finfer, who ran
the Universal distribution company in Philadelphia. They
also owned the Jamie/Guyden label, and distributed Goldner's Gone label locally. Phil wasn't very happy with them,
so he terminated the arrangement and hired Danny Davis,
whom he'd met as National Promotion Manager for Hill
and Range and Big Top Records. Danny had been brought
to Screen Gems by Donny Kirshner, but was quick to grab
the new job: "Phil made me what I considered to be a
fantastic offer. He made me a Vice-President. . . . The label
was really only Phil and myself. He got tougher after I
joined. He went into his own set up, leaving Universal
because he felt they'd done him for some money. So he
offered his distribution around the industry."

For Phil, this was the beginning of his victory over

the industry. They'd always looked on him like he was some kind of freak, a nut who would either crack and knuckle under or just disappear.

"When I decided to make my own label, they all said it couldn't be done," he remembers. "They said I wouldn't get paid by the distributors. I was friendly with George Goldner, and a lot of the people who really made the record industry, and I had lots of talks with them. I said, 'They tell me I won't get paid if I open up a label,' and they said, 'You'll get paid if you make a lot of hits, and you don't give them the follow-up until they pay you for the previous one.'

"So I never thought to myself, 'What a silly way to make a living' . . . you know, to have to threaten someone with your new record if they don't pay you for the old one. It was just automatic, until later on I began to think how stupid it was.

"After I'd made about eight or ten (hits) in a row I started to get paid regularly, and I had no problems, but somebody said, 'Phil, if you make great records, you could put them out from Mexico and they're gonna sell' . . . so I bought my own pressing plant, and made my own distributors." (It may be significant that the later Philles pressings are often poor quality, with abominable surface noise.)

Spector felt he was fighting the established industry, and quite consciously refused all attempts at rapprochement. "I never pressed with a major label, I'd never do anything with the majors . . . I did everything on my own. It was rough and it was hard, but it just seemed very natural at the time."

Rough and hard it was, as Danny Davis testifies: "Phil was making so much money that a lot of people owed him, and he had a tough time collecting. He became very tough, and wasted no time in letting people know that he'd sue 'em. He knew they needed him if they wanted to do business, but he wasn't going to service them until he got paid for the last lot. He was always being done in by distributors . . . even now, I'm sure that some people still owe him stuff from the heyday of Philles."

Against this vicious background Spector was trying to make great records. The strain must have been immense. It showed itself in every context of his life—not just when he went to the supermarket and found people complaining about his hair, and not just the backbiting of people who resented his not depending on them for his success, but at work too.

Tony Orlando remembers going to a session at Mirasound just for the pleasure of watching Phil create. "Mirasound was a really dingy place, but a good studio. I think Brooks Arthur was the engineer that day—he used Brooks a lot. He was just cutting tracks, but when he cut tracks the whole orchestra was there. It sounded fantastic to me, it sounded incredible. I came back the next day and I asked Brooks how it went, and he said 'Phil scrapped the whole date.' He didn't like it, and he was going back to the West Coast to cut it again. That whole date was gone.

"What I remember from that session is the musicians not really respecting Phil. I was very young at the time, but I do remember that there was a guitar player on the date named Charlie Macey . . . Carole [King] used him a lot. The guys in the studio on that particular day were really straight . . . I mean, in '61 they weren't young kids. I remember Charlie Macey saying, 'What is it with this nut? What is he trying to do?' Because Phil's whole technique was against the grain of most recording. His whole approach was different, and this one particular musician, who was used on most of the dates in those days, didn't really understand Phil."

The guitarist's attitude was not uncommon among the musicians Phil was forced to work with in New York. The tightly closed shop at sessions may be what drove him to record on the West Coast. The next Crystals record, "He's A Rebel," was his first recording at the Gold Star Studios in Hollywood, and after that he never made another record in New York as long as Philles lasted.

In Hollywood, Phil found session men who were much younger than their New York counterparts, and far more amenable to his revolutionary ideas. The list of names he used on the sessions—and he was the first pop producer to credit these previously faceless men by name on all his subsequent album covers—now looks like a list of today's superstars.

On keyboards he used Leon Russell, now the member of a peer group which includes his close friends Bob Dylan, George Harrison, and Joe Cocker; Larry Knechtel, a former Rebel with Duane Eddy who later went on to play on the Mama's and Papa's records; Harold Battiste, a big man from New Orleans who'd recorded Barbara George's "I Know" for his own AFO label, and would later mastermind the records of Sonny and Cher and Doctor John The Night Tripper; and Don Randi, who in his own right brought cocktail jazz piano to a new and superflorid height.

Knechtel also played bass on these sessions, alongside Jimmy Bond, a fine musician who appeared on many excellent jazz albums, and Ray Pohlman. The guitars were Barney Kessel, one of the half dozen most influential jazzmen on his instrument since the Second World War; Glen

Campbell, about whom everybody knows; and several top session players including Billy Strange, Bill Pitman, Tommy Tedesco, and Carole Kaye, a lady who also played bass and actually wrote tutors for that instrument.

On percussion were Sonny Bono, who worshipped Phil; Frank Capp, another solid jazz musician; Julius Wechter, and Gene Estes. The horns included the abovementioned Steve Douglas, plus jazz tenorist Jay Migliori and trombonist Lou Blackburn, who led a jazz quintet with trumpeter Freddie Hill at the time.

Last, and also first, were the drummers. In the beginning there was Hal Blaine, who virtually created a

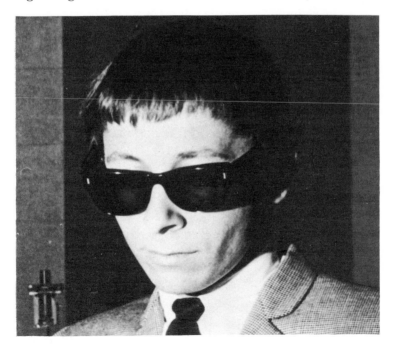

Jack Nitzsche, the arranger Spector found when he moved to Hollywood. Phil could do the job himself, but having an arranger "made it lots easier."

style by himself and became an elder statesman among West Coast session percussionists. He was later replaced by Earl Palmer, whom Phil liked even more because "he had better time." Ultimately, Ritchie Frost was brought in to play a second kit alongside Palmer.

Nino Tempo played pretty much everything: piano, percussion, tenor sax (he made an album as a tenorist, with a rather polite trio). He'd already made his first hit record with April Stevens on Atco—"Sweet And Lovely"—and later, in '63, they had a number one smash, "Deep Purple."

Finally, Spector discovered Jack Nitzsche who, besides playing keyboards and rattling things, became Phil's regular arranger. Spector had an unusual if practical conception of the arranger's function: "I know how to arrange, I do my own arrangements, but it's much easier to have someone to write it out than to have to sit down and do it yourself. It takes too much time, and then you have to change it all at the session anyway. I wrote down every note, and then just had (the arranger) do the actual writing and block the chords out, so they'd know how to change it when I was at the studio. In the studio, I'd say 'Change it—make everybody a third higher' and they'd do that stuff. It made it lots easier."

"He's A Rebel" was Nitzsche's first Spector session. Phil found him "really good and cooperative and I always used him. Then he disappeared before we made 'Lovin' Feelin',' and I guess he really felt unimportant when he saw that we could do it without him, that it could be any arranger. It was his own fault, because he was gone." But that jumps the gun by a couple of years.

The other man Spector found at Gold Star was his engineer, Larry Levine. When Phil went in to cut "He's A Rebel," the studio's regular engineer, Stan Ross, was on holiday, and Levine, then "the stock-boy or something" according to Spector, was delegated to take his place.

Levine himself says: "I knew that Phil had worked at Atlantic and with the Drifters, and when I walked into a session of that magnitude I was a little nervous. . . . I thought I was going to blow it. I was a little frightened by the new sound, and I didn't get a good feeling from Phil. He looked like a creepy kid to me. But eventually we worked up an understanding."

He can say that again. After "He's A Rebel," the tall, raw-boned Levine engineered every record Phil Spector made for the next eight years.

"Larry's a nice fellow, really sweet," says Phil. "You really needed somebody good alongside of you, and Larry was really helpful, really good. And in those days, for what I was doing, he was invaluable. Everything was an experiment. We were breaking every rule there was to break, like 'don't go over the red line with the needle' and 'watch this' and 'it's gonna skip' . . . and who cares? Just make the record."

Although "He's A Rebel" was a Crystals record according to the label, no Crystal sang lead. Instead it was taken by a girl called Darlene Love, whom Phil had found singing background on sessions in Los Angeles. It was one of the most important discoveries he ever made.

Darlene, although no teenager, had a peculiarly young voice, which made it suitable for the songs Phil liked best—the ones dealing with adolescent emotional experiences. However, unlike most kids around, she was also a solidly professional singer with exemplary technique, control, and flexibility. From Spector's point of view, she could do exactly what he wanted in terms of vocal phrasing and inflection. He wouldn't have to go through each four-bar phrase with her a million times, as he'd had to with most of the kids he'd been producing for the past couple of years. In a word, Darlene was a godsend: when Spector, reminiscing in 1971, commented that she was "a big talent," one could tell by his tone of voice that he *really* meant it.

"He's A Rebel" was written by Gene Pitney. The year before Pitney had written "Hello Mary Lou" for Ricky Nelson. Now he hit big with this one too. It is a classic song now, the all-time definition of the rebel boy who only shows his tender side to his girl when the two are alone. (When I first heard this one I was 15 years old, and it sounded like an anthem. It still does.) Darlene sings with just the right amount of girlish defiance. Those "no-no-no" bits in the chorus, the double-time handclapping at the end, the wild piano hammering, a beautifully shaped baritone sax solo, and the baritone who spends his time underlining and reinforcing the bass line—all bring a new depth to the record.

With "I Love You Eddie" on the B side, "He's A Rebel" became Philles' first number one hit in October, 1962. It must have been a sweet moment for the label's president, sitting in his penthouse in the Park Sutton, overlooking the East River at 440 East 62nd Street. He had won. But it wasn't the end of anything at all. He felt like he hadn't even started.

Throughout his career and even to this day, Spector has had to prove that he is the best—and long after he'd proved it conclusively to the rest of the world, he still had to keep demonstrating it to himself. Something, goodness knows what it was, would not let him rest. He put analysts on the job, even two at once, but I very much doubt if any of them discovered the key.

Spector now had a number one hit to follow up. He did it in a typically unconventional way. He put together a group from some of the LA background singers: Darlene and another girl called Fanita James, both members of a back-up trio called The Blossoms, and a guy by the name of Bobby Sheen, a tall fellow with his hair in a peaked, pointy process, whom Phil liked because "he sang like Clyde McPhatter"—the Drifter's first lead singer.

He called them Bob B. Soxx and the Blue Jeans. When he referred to them in interviews he would say, "That really is his name, you know!"

The first song the new group cut was the old hit tune "Zip-A-Dee-Doo-Dah"—an unlikely vehicle for Pop R & B if there ever was one. But Phil made it into something else again. That record contained many seeds of the sound which was to emerge.

It was a strange session. Things were moving okay, but after a couple of hours, Larry and Phil had the feeling that something, somewhere, was wrong which they couldn't put their fingers on. For a start, Phil didn't like the sound of the saxophone solo. He told the saxophonist to stop playing and ordered Billy Strange to take the solo instead on guitar.

Larry picks up the story: "We'd spent two and a half hours recording it, and my dials were jumping all over the place. So I switched everything off and Phil said, 'What're you doing?' I told him that I had to start again, right from scratch."

So while Phil supervised, Larry started switching the instrument mikes back on, one by one, from the percussion through the basses and rhythm guitars to the keyboards.

At point Strange's guitar was the only instrument not miked. But his monitor speaker in the studio was itself so loud that it leaked into everybody else's mikes. It produced the craziest sound: metallic, distant, as if he were playing in the next room with the door shut.

"That's it!" screamed Phil. Quite by accident, they

had stumbled across a noise that no one had ever heard before. There were plenty of people who still remember when, hearing the guitar solo on that cut for the first time, they muttered in sheer awe "What's *that*?"

"You know there's no drum on that record," Phil says. "There's just a bass drum. A lot of those records didn't have any drum because I couldn't get a drum sound. Today I don't spend that much time thinking about it, but in those days if I couldn't get a drum sound I'd go crazy. I'd go out of my mind, spend five or six hours, trying to get a drum sound, and it's really hard on the musicians because they're just playing the same thing over and over. But I figured . . . I just tried to imagine one mike over everything, how it would be."

One mike over everything. Nobody has ever managed to define the Spector Sound with any real accuracy, but that little phrase comes closer than any I've heard.

"Zip-A-Dee-Doo-Dah" also boasted Phil's first real "Spector B side," a genre which would later become notorious. Spector would write a little riff and just have the sessionmen blow on it in their usually half-hearted jamming style. Each little blow lasted about two minutes, enough for a cut. He would then give the numbers silly names: "Nino and Sonny (Big Trouble)," or "Chubby Danny D." (Danny Davis, of course), or "Dr. Kaplan's Office" (Spector's analyst?) or "Bebe And Susu" (the Ronettes' mothers), or "Annette" (the name of Spector's first wife, married in the early sixties and divorced two or three years later).

These B sides were created to force the focus totally on the top deck. Sometimes disk jockeys would flip records, for variety or because they didn't like the A side. With commendably sharp business acumen, Phil decided that he couldn't afford to lose even one play on any of his

BOB-B-SOXX and the BLUE JEANS

BOBBY   DARLENE   FANITA

Darlene Love sang lead on many of Spector's early Los Angeles productions for his Philles label, including the Crystals' "He's A Rebel" and Bob B. Soxx and the Blue Jeans' "Zip-A-Dee-Doo-Dah." In the top picture, Darlene is flanked by Bobby Sheen and Fanita James.

records. So the DJ's had to play the A side, because no one was going to listen to some fast-fingered guitarist jetting through jazz changes at 90 bars a minute.

Nowadays, these B sides have engendered their own parlor game. Who, for instance, is "Big Red" on the flip side of Philles 120? And who are the Harry and Milt who meet Hal Blaine on Philles 119?

Had it been at all possible, Phil would have preferred to put out single-sided records—his solution was, thus, the next best thing, even if it didn't make for particularly good value to the poor consumer, who never could quite believe that it was really the Ronettes, as billed, playing guitars on "Tedesco And Pitman."

"Zip-A-Dee-Doo-Dah" was, incidentally, the first Philles record to bear, in that space between grooves and label, the hand-scratched legend "Phil & Annette." It appeared on a dozen consecutive singles, ceasing, rather poignantly, after its final appearance on the Ronettes' "Baby I Love You." Annette, the wife mentioned earlier, was a couple of years younger than Phil and a psychology student at Hunter College in New York. Curiously enough, the original girl singer with the Teddy Bears, whose name was also Annette, was also a couple of years younger than Phil and, according to the notes on the group's album, had also been considering psychology as a career. Both girls have been described, quite independently, as "very bright." It seems hard to believe, but none of Phil's closest friends in the business at that time know whether or not both Annettes were in fact the same girl. Not Paul Case, who was almost a father-figure to him, and not even Elaine Orlando, who was Phil's secretary for a time and who reputedly ran errands for his wife upon occasion. It is perhaps good to have a few mysteries around.

After the "Zip-A-Dee-Doo-Dah" success, Phil just

kept piling strength upon strength. At 23 years of age he was making vast amounts of money, and getting weirder and weirder. He had started to hire bodyguards, as a result of his long-established paranoia over the possibility of physical assault.

"I think it's part of the sickness of being a genius," says Tony Orlando. "He was so creative . . . it was so much demanded of him to be an extrovert, and he's not. He's really very inward-looking and shy. It's difficult for him to live up to what everybody expects him to be, and every day he had to do it. After all of that fighting constantly against his inferiority complexes, he eventually began to believe it, that people were out to get him, to beat him up or kill him. In essence, I guess they were out to get him . . . in some way, whether it be his money or whether it be his fragile little body. He was a giant . . . and he's just a tiny little man, he looks like he could break in half if you just blew on him. So he did have bodyguards, and they were big, huge."

Phil's bodyguards became legendary. The fact that he felt he needed them at all astonished the British press when he visited London in 1964. Tony Hall, then promo man for British Decca, who handled Phil's product, vividly remembers a visit to Hollywood during Phil's "Japanese period," when he was surrounded by black belt karate experts. "He had all these silent musclemen, and he never went anywhere without them. I went to the Daisy, a club in LA, one night, and it was so awful that I phoned Phil and asked him to get me out. He turned up with *five* of these heavies to rescue me . . . anybody who looked at him, he'd go up to them and stare straight into their eyes. It scared them stiff."

And all the time, the sound was getting bigger. Listening to his records in sequence, one can't miss it—each

one is just a little broader, a little thicker, a little more
mind-destroying than the one before.

The real breakthrough came between April and
August, 1963, when he released three records that supplied
unequivocal evidence of a man who was doing something
genuinely new with pop music. At the time nobody thought
about it too much. The records were accepted as great
pop hits, just something a little different about them. But,
as time proved, they were more than that.

The first of these three records came from the Crystals again. Now solidly entrenched as a regular hit group
("He's Sure The Boy I Love," the follow-up to "Rebel,"
had made number 11), they released in April a record
called "Da Doo Ron Ron," written by Phil with the new
team of Jeff Barry and Ellie Greenwich. Another husband-
and-wife combination, Jeff and Ellie had constituted a
group called the Raindrops, who made a couple of decent-
sized hits on Jubilee prior to Jeff's already noted composition of "Tell Laura I Love Her" for Ray Peterson (and
"Chip Chip" for Gene McDaniels at Liberty). As writers,
Jeff and Ellie were now signed to Leiber and Stoller.

When writing with other people, Phil describes his
function as that of "a steering wheel. They would get 'feels'
and ideas, riffs and melody lines, and we'd build upon
it. They'd write ten sets of lyrics, and I'd pick the best
one. It was like working with the arrangers, it made it
easier. I only worked with a few sets (of writers) that were
really good: Barry and Cynthia, Carole and Gerry, and
then Jeff and Ellie . . . it was more important that they
understood me than anything else. Jeff and Ellie *really*
understood me, really knew what I wanted, and were able
to deliver. The others understood, but not as much as
Jeff and Ellie did."

"Da Doo Ron Ron" was a perfect confirmation of

that understanding. A faster tempo than anything he'd done until then, it simply exploded out of record players everywhere. The saxes blatted, the piano chimed madly, the drums raced—and this time it was a *real* Crystal, Lala Brooks, who took the lead with almost as much assurance as Darlene. The words were great and just this side of inane—best of all, it was instantly catchy.

"Then He Kissed Me," the Crystals' next record, took it one step further. This time a tympani bore down on the first beat of every bar, castanets clicked to a new and inexorable rhythm, and somewhere in the background you could feel the sound of a whole gang of guitars. On top of that were strings, still slightly Driftersish, but now on their way to a more ethereal sound.

But the last of the trilogy was the real skull-cruncher, the song that finally brought about the revolution: "Be My Baby" by the Ronettes.

This group, three girls, had made some records before they met Phil. They had been known as Ronnie and the Ronettes and had appeared around New York. Tony Orlando had taken Ronnie to see Donny Kirshner around 1962. They had made some singles and an album for Colpix, of which "I'm On The Wagon" (Colpix 646) is a typically awful example. At that point they showed nothing to suggest anything other than mediocrity.

How Phil met them remains a point of some dispute. It may be that Donny introduced them, or, as Ronnie tells it, she got a wrong number on the telephone one night, and the wrong number was Phil, who discovered that she sang with a group and so asked her to come down and sing backgrounds for him the next night. It's all passed into legend now.

When the Ronettes made their appearance with "Be My Baby" in August, it was immediately obvious that they

The Ronettes. From top: Estelle Bennett, Nedra Talley, Veronica Bennett.

were to the bright, chirpy little Crystals what Elvis was to Pat Boone.

The Ronettes were two sisters—Veronica (Ronnie) and Estelle Bennett, 19 and 20 respectively—and their 18-year-old cousin, Nedra Talley. They wore massively sculptured bouffants, piled about 18 inches high, but it was the eyes that made the real impact. They were positively daubed with black mascara—the year the Ronettes hit the chart, Helena Rubinstein's profits probably doubled. They looked dangerous, a threat to any average male's self-esteem, but despite the challenge in their eyes they performed love songs in which they pleaded with their boys: "Be My Baby," "Baby I Love You," "Do I Love You," "Oh I Love You," "Is This What I Get For Loving You," and so on. This marvellously piquant contrast between promise and performance was made possible because lead singer Ronnie possessed, or was possessed by, a hugely quavering voice, the like of which no one had heard before. She had one of the few real pop voices—you couldn't imagine her singing any other kind of song than the sort Phil put before her.

"Be My Baby" was cataclysmic. The orchestra, outrageously gigantic, had pianos and basses arrayed in ranks in the studios, and everyone joining in to play the percussion which Spector had arranged with almost militaristic precision. The recording roared straight up to number two—Brian Wilson reckons it the best record Spector ever made.

How on earth did Spector ever envision this kind of controlled noise?

"I always went in for that Wagnerian approach to rock and roll."

Had he any formal grounding in classical music?

"Just self-grounding."

But had he heard Wagner?

"Oh, very much so. Very influenced by it. It's hard to imagine, really, because rock and roll is such a . . . everyone looks down on it, it's just rock and roll. But if you listen to the immensity of one Wagner record, and then you put on one old 'Then He Kissed Me' or something, you can *hear* that there's a student of the school there, just playing different chords and stuff."

Spector once described what he was doing as "writing little symphonies for the kids." He was consciously trying to make something *good*, as well as rock and roll.

"Always . . . it was much more important than success. The fact that it was successful was just icing on the cake. It wasn't the main purpose at all. It was always to try and write something that was good, and moving, and important. Because if I didn't make anything that was *better*, I might as well have left it to Fats Domino, because he did it all, by himself. The business didn't need me to come along. I had to progress, make things much better. 'Little Star' by the Elegants . . . I mean, that was *great*; what need was there for Phil Spector to come along and make his records unless they were going to be a contribution and really do something more? I hope they did, anyway. That would be good, if they did."

Jeff Barry, who was there most of the time, describes the evolutionary process of a Spector record of the period:

"It was basically a formula. Jack Nitzsche was the arranger, and I think besides any particular melodic riffs that Phil desired, Jack could have written what Phil would have wanted. You're going to have four or five guitars lined up, gut-string guitars, and they're going to follow the chords, nothing tricky. You're going to use two basses in fifths, with the same type of line, and the strings . . . well, Jack could design his own string arrangements, although at times there were melodic things that we wanted them to do, so we'd sing 'em to him.

"There might be certain breaks that Phil had come up with, or we'd come up with, and those would be written out. But by and large there was a formula arrangement to create a formula sound, which you can hear develop if you play all the records in sequence. There would be seven horns, adding the little punches, and there would be the formula percussion instruments—the little bells, the shakers, and tambourines. Then he used his own formula for echo, and overtone effects with the strings."

By autumn of '63 the Philles' sound was well established by the records of the Crystals, Ronettes, and Darlene Love (who had made three superb solo efforts), all of which reached the Top 60.

Phil had still another idea though. Maybe what triggered it off was all those little tinkling bells he'd been using. He wanted to make a Christmas album. It sounds like a terrible, corny idea, but Phil knew different: playing on that sentimental core hidden inside his freakiness, he decided he wanted to take all the usual Christmas songs, and, using all of his artists, really do them over differently.

It was nearly the all-time white elephant. The album took months to make, because Spector was trying really hard this time. It wasn't going to be one of those ordinary albums: two hit singles plus ten pieces of junk. It was going to be "good, moving, and important."

Barry and Levine remember the sessions with a shudder. Levine: "It went on for months, and I never wanted to see him again after that. Day and night for months. . . ." Barry: "I stood there for days and days and days, just playing shakers."

Against all the odds, it turned out a great aesthe-

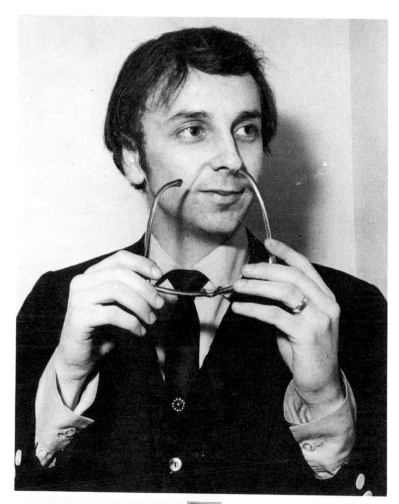

Phil Spector and his Christmas Album: eight years later, people were paying $25 for a copy.

tic success: Phil had taken all these shoddy little songs like "Frosty The Snowman" and "Santa Claus Is Coming To Town" and "Rudolph The Red Nosed Reindeer" and made them into great rock and roll and great art.

What's more, he had truly captured the spirit of Christmas—cynics may laugh, but just *listen* to the Ronettes' "Sleigh Ride," to the care with which it is produced: the bells and horses' hooves, and the way Ronnie sounds like she's singing from inside a big fur coat. *Listen* to "The Bells Of St. Mary," on which Bobby Sheen sings his McPhatterish heart out over one of Nitzsche's most brainstorming arrangements, with an occasional wild interjection from Darlene.

The whole album is like that—good from the start to the finish. Then, on the final track, Spector approaches the microphone and says, in his high little voice: "Hello, this is Phil Spector. It is so difficult at this time to say words that would express my feelings about the album to which you have just listened . . . an album that has been in the planning for many, many months. First, let me thank all the people who have worked so hard with me in the production of this album, and in my endeavor and desire to bring something new and different to the music of Christmas, and to the record industry which is so much a part of my life. Of course, the biggest thanks goes to you, for giving me the opportunity to relate my feelings of Christmas through the music that I love. At this moment, I am very proud of all the artists, and on behalf of all of them—the Crystals, the Ronettes, Darlene Love, Bob B. Soxx and the Blue Jeans, and myself—may we wish you the very merriest of Christmases and the happiest of New Years. . . . And thank you so very much for letting us spend this Christmas with you." The choir then sings a final chorus of "Silent Night," over muted strings which positively throb with Yuletide goodwill.

Some people find that appalling. I think he meant it. Whichever, copies of *A Christmas Gift To You*, never a great seller in its time, now change hands for 25 dollars and upwards in New York.

⸘

About this time, Phil contemplated starting a new label—Phil Spector Records. Danny Davis explains: "I think the 'Les' part of Philles had started to tarnish a little for him. He's quite an ego-man, and he thought that maybe just by calling the label Phil Spector Records he could get people to listen. All his things were ballyhooed as 'the new Spector record,' and the artist was hardly mentioned."

Two records were put out on this label: one by a group called the Imaginations, and a solo record by Veronica. The latter, called "Why Don't They Let Us Fall In Love," was a very acceptable little record, but neither of them did anything when released and are both believed to have been withdrawn.

Davis: "We tested the Veronica record on several markets, but it never showed. We used to do that if there was some question about a record—we'd take a shot with it in a particular area, where we knew the market. If it succeeded, we'd try to spread it to markets which were basically similar to the test area."

Phil also tried to start a label called Annette—two releases were recorded, once again without any success. One of these records has a curious history: "I Love You Ringo" by Bonnie Jo Mason, was scheduled to become Annette 1001. The song had been the idea of Paul Case. (Case had recently given Phil a couple of very promising young writers called Pete Andreoli, shortened to Anders, and Vinnie Poncia. Doc Pomus had brought

One of the two releases on the Phil
Spector Records label, with Jeff
Barry, who co-wrote this and many
other songs with his wife, Ellie
Greenwich, and Spector.

them to Case, who signed them as writers to Hill and Range,
then passed them on to Phil. Earlier with a group in Provi-
dence, they were now living in New York. Together, they
made a monster record for the Red Bird label under the
name of the Tradewinds: "New York's A Lonely Town"
(RB 10-020), which reached number 32 early in '65.) Case
had been watching the success of the Beatles, and noticed
that Ringo was the one who seemed to draw most attention
from the fans. He suggested to Phil that Spector, Anders,
and Poncia write a song called "I Love You Ringo."

They did, but the problem remained: who
should sing it? Phil had an idea. For some months, Sonny
Bono had been pulling his coat about some chick he was
going with, a chick with long black hair who could *really*

sing. Sonny wanted to produce her for Philles—or wanted Phil to produce her, or just *anything.* So Phil thought: why not give the Ringo song to Sonny's chick?

Spector recorded it with her, and released it under her name: Bonnie Jo Mason. She later became Cher.

Like Ronnie's solo record, "I Love You Ringo" was tested in a few regional markets. Nothing happened, so it was quietly forgotten.

The only other record on Annette was a really strange one: "Uncle Kev" backed with "Oh Baby," by Harvey and Doc with The Dwellers. Harvey must have been Phil, but who were Doc and The Dwellers? Bill Millar describes "Uncle Kev" as "three minutes of guitar solo, all on one note. You play it for laughs only."

Spector called his third subsidiary label Phi-Dan. It was set up for a very specific purpose: to share some of his glory with Danny Davis. Davis says: "It was one of the nicest things he's ever done. He wanted to give me a piece of the action, because I didn't have a piece of the Philles action—I was on a salary. He also thought that we could capitalize on my winning the industry's Promotion Man of the Year award two years running, in '64 and '65. He thought we'd be assured of airplay if my name was linked with it, because of my good relationships with the disk jockeys. It didn't work out that way, because the DJ's only play what's in the grooves, and obviously we didn't have it. We had about three releases, none of which managed to duplicate the success we had with Philles.

"Phil did a lot of nice things for me. If I needed a car, he'd buy me one, and he also paid for my move out to California. He was a very strange guy, but if he got fond of you there was no end to what he'd do for you." According to Davis, the records on Phi-Dan were all made by permutations of the various backing groups he was using in Hollywood. Scheduled releases included records by Florence DeVore, Betty Willis, and Bonnie and the Treasures—the latter record, "Home of the Brave," actually made the chart in August '65, when it crawled up to the 77th spot. This one was actually a tremendous record, a Mann/Weil song with a lyric again referring back to that old rebel character, which asks of America: "Home of the brave, land of the free, why won't you let him be what he wants to be?" It is a minor classic of High School pop, wih a little girl lead singer and a really huge sound.

But it didn't take off. Instead it marked the end of Phil's efforts to establish a new label—efforts, suggests Paul Case, which may have been prompted by the feeling he had too many releases on Philles. Like the majors, he decided to create another division, thus making sure that one label wasn't going to show all the time on station programmers' lists. But in the end he had to stick with the Philles logo.

≀

The English invasion of '64 and '65 appealed greatly to Phil, and he got involved in it very quickly. Unlike the rest of the industry, which treated the Beatles as a threat to their established control, he realized that these performers were on *his* wavelength: young, aware, and with their own hands on the reins.

He got to know the Beatles quickly. Later on, the Ronettes appeared with them on one very memorable British package-show tour.

But at that time he got on best with the Rolling Stones—and particularly with their manager, Andrew Oldham. Oldham was the prototype of the new breed of British pop tastemaker: very young, very sharp, and very ex-Public School hip. Oldham worshipped Spector then, time and was trying very hard to be like him: he had started to become weird, and surrounded himself with heavies at all times. Phil also liked Oldham a great deal. When Phil visited Britain they would share wild times together. People in London treated Phil like a human being—they didn't try to grab handfuls of his hair in supermarkets.

Tony Hall remembers driving around London with Phil in a chauffeured Rolls-Royce very late one night. They were rolling up Curzon Street, in super-rich Mayfair, when Phil suddenly asked the driver to stop, get out, and find him a bottle of milk.

"As soon as the driver was out, Phil leapt into the front seat and started off," Hall says. "He got into first gear instead of reverse, and hit the front of a bank. The Rolls was lurching all over the place . . . and we ended up with Phil, this little mad monster wearing the driver's peaked cap, roaring down the Mall towards Buckingham Palace—*on the pavement*. There were some policemen there, and they couldn't understand what was going on . . . they just stood there shaking their heads, and didn't do anything. All those stories about Phil are true, and that one's typical."

Hall organized the party at which Phil and the Ronettes first met the Beatles. It took place at Hall's home. The atmosphere started out a little strained—Phil went out for a while, then came back at three o'clock in the morning, and started telling the stories behind his hit records. After that they all got on fine.

Phil actually participated in a couple of Stones sessions. He co-wrote "Little By Little" with Mick Jagger, played maraccas on the same song (Gene Pitney is on piano), and played guitar on "Play With Fire," which was recorded in America.

There was also the session, famous among the

Spector, being interviewed on British television by compere Keith Fordyce, in 1964.

Stones' intimates, at which they taped a song dedicated to Sir Edward Lewis, elderly head of Decca, the Stones' British record company. The group, plus Andrew and Phil, sing on this record. It is reported by all who have heard it to be startlingly obscene. It was never released, and there are only a very few copies in existence.

Phil had good reason to like London: when he arrived he was featured on a center spread in the five-million-circulation *Daily Mirror*, with a reverential story; when he appeared on the TV pop show *Ready, Steady,*

Go! he was treated as if he were somebody of importance, not just another maniacal little ego-freak.

When the Beatles and Stones visited LA, Phil enjoyed showing them around Hollywood, and taking them to Martoni's, a Sunset Boulevard watering hole frequented by showbiz people, columnists, and people in the music business. They were like him: they had style, and they *understood*. Not like all those gross hustlers he had been dealing with up to now, who puffed on their Havanas and guzzled burgers.

He was very happy.

≀

In the middle of 1964, Spector met a duo called the Righteous Brothers. The group embodied several contradictions. To begin with, they weren't brothers—they were Bill Medley and Bobby Hatfield. Secondly, although they sang with a pure black sound and inflection, they were in fact white. Their explanation for this was that, when they started, they played a lot of black clubs, and were heavily influenced by their surroundings.

Medley came from Los Angeles, Hatfield from Beaver Dam, Wisconsin. They were both 24 years old, and before meeting Phil they'd cut a good number of records for the Moonglow lable. Half a dozen of them had reached the Hot 100, and their first, "Little Latin Lupe Lu," had even made number 49. They were a good minor league act with a respectable track record. No one could have rightly expected much more from them.

Except Phil Spector, who was true to his habit of favoring comparative unknowns—he just wasn't interested in anybody who'd tasted success before he signed them. "They came to me, and I thought they were great, terrific. They were white, but they understood black singing."

Presumably his signing them also had something to do with the slightly diminishing power of Philles as a chart force in '64. His last five records before the Righteous Brothers only made it to 92, 39, 34, 98, and 23. Not satisfactory.

Every Philles record to date had featured a black singer—perhaps he felt that, to break through again, he needed a white artist or group. Still, he'd always put his faith in the black vocal sound, and he wasn't about to compromise it. The act he finally picked perfectly combined all the necessary virtues.

Barry Mann, whose writing partnership with his wife, Cynthia Weil, produced many hits. Of them all, the greatest was "You've Lost That Lovin' Feelin'," co-written with Spector.

Phil got together with Barry Mann and Cynthia Weil specifically to write a song for the duo. Before long, they all realized that this was going to be *the* record—the one which finally attained all the musical goals he'd ever set for himself. It would have everything; it would be the most lavish, most perfect production ever conceived.

They spent months working on the record. "I hoped it was going to be that record, I really did," says Spector. "I really loved it."

When it came out, it put the world flat on its back. There must be thousands of people scattered all over who can remember exactly where they were, and exactly what they were doing, at the moment they first heard "You've Lost That Lovin' Feelin'," by the Righteous Brothers.

Medley starts the song, that gaunt and hungry deep voice riding a half-submerged bass line, and one by one the instruments and backing voices enter, until Hatfield comes in for the first chorus. There follows that hanging riff, with ghostly vibes on top. The strings join in for the second verse: by this time Medley is wailing; by the chorus they are both reaching for the high notes. They trade phrases for the bridge—Hatfield backed by an echoing bongo—before building to a climax which recasts the elements of Gospel music into a new kind of catharsis.

The track is immaculate. Arranged by Gene Page (Nitzsche, as Phil said earlier, had just disappeared), it finally created that "wall of sound" that Spector had been looking for. Only two or three years after the record's appearance did fans start hearing the separate instruments: before that, the track existed as an undifferentiated mass of sound, impossible to break down and analyze into separate components.

The rest of the world shared Phil's enthusiasm for the record. "The timing was right," he says. "The people who were ready for it really broke it and got onto it, and *wanted* it to be a hit."

But it wasn't all easy. Checking the timing of the record on the original Philles label, one notices that the record's playtime is listed at three minutes and five seconds. It is really much longer of course—all of 40 seconds longer. Phil had seen that timing put on the label on purpose, fearing that radio programmers might be disinclined to play a record that was 3.45 long, no matter how good it was. And he couldn't afford to take any risks with this one.

The ploy almost backfired. Danny Davis recalls: "Some of the New York stations wouldn't play it, after they'd checked the timing on their own clocks. Sometimes, when they played it the first time, it went wrong . . . you know, they'd have a News feed coming up, and they'd play the record, and it was so long that they'd miss the News. And they wouldn't play it again."

But nothing could stop the record. By Christmas it was the national Number One. Everybody was talking about it, for it represented the scaling of a new musical peak.

In Britain, the record was "covered" by a Liverpool girl called Cilla Black, an early friend of the Beatles. By this time Cilla was solidly established as a regular domestic chart name. Everything she did made the Top Ten, and no one imagined she'd do anything different on this one. She had shortened the song because "she didn't want people to get bored."

But enough Britons were hip to the Righteous Brothers' version to get it played also, and a "chart war" commenced. Cilla's version leapt in first. When the Righteous Brothers made their first appearance, many places below her, it seemed to be all over. The local girl had won.

However, there was to be no reckoning without Andrew Oldham. The World's Number One Phil Spector Fan took out advertising space in all the music papers, exhorting people to buy the original version. He even used the Philles slogan: "Tomorrow's Sound Today."

Nobody will ever know for sure whether it was

YOU'VE LOST THAT LOVIN' FEELING

THE RIGHTEOUS BROTHERS

This advert. is not for commercial gain, it is taken as something that must be said about the great new PHIL SPECTOR Record, THE RIGHTEOUS BROTHERS singing "YOU'VE LOST THAT LOVIN' FEELING". Already in the American Top Ten, this is Spector's greatest production, the last word in Tomorrow's sound Today, exposing the overall mediocrity of the Music Industry.

Signed

Andrew Oldham

P.S. See them on this week's READY, STEADY, GO

Andrew Oldham's ad, in the *Melody Maker,* **which probably helped to make the Righteous Brothers' record a hit in Britain.**

Oldham's move which tipped the scales, but it certainly set the scene buzzing. On January 30, 1965, the Righteous Brothers leapfrogged over Cilla and zoomed a straight eighteen places up to number one. Cilla, it was reported, cabled her congratulations to the Brothers. It was one of those very rare occasions in the pop world when sheer good taste had carried the day.

Spector believes that "Lovin' Feelin'" was the peak of Philles. "You know, you don't make anything in the record business that lasts very long," he says, "and when a record like that lasts a long time, it's really startling, because you don't have any Academy Awards for it. If you make a movie that lasts two hours, it goes on and on and on. It's just nice to know that some people think that out of all the records ever made, that might be the very best, and that's ... *good*, y' know. I used to bring people into the studio and play that record just to watch their reactions, just to see what happened to them. That happened to have been a very good song, anyway. We wrote a very good song at that time."

ξ

It was during this epoch that the famous airplane incident took place which is dramatized by Tom Wolfe in his essay.

Jeff Barry and Ellie Greenwich accompanied Phil on the plane that day. There is still a certain awe in Barry's voice, seven years later, when he recounts the tale:

"We were going back from Los Angeles to New York, and we were on the plane, waiting, boarded ... plane's loaded. I was sitting across the aisle from Phil, and he leans over to me and says, 'Hey man, I don't think I can make it.' Does his Ahmet Ertegun imitation. And says, 'Hey ... it's filling up ... I don't know. Look there,

The Righteous Brothers (Bobby Hatfield, left, and Bill Medley), and the jacket of their fourth single, "Ebb Tide."

Jeffrey, all the way in the back, it's filling up . . . people
. . . losers.' So I said yeah, that's it, and he says, 'I gotta
get off. Miss, I gotta get off this plane.' And he's flying
. . . he's always on pills when he's flying, and he's flying
before he's flying. So the stewardess went up front and
evidently the pilot gave permission to let this guy off.

"Phil gets off, and Ellie and I sit there, and
I think, Phil Spector's too bright. I don't wanna bet against
Phil Spector. *Let's get off the plane.* So we raised our hands
also, and asked to be excused. All these fairly straight
people were sitting there, and I had a two-day growth
of beard because we'd been in the studio, and Phil looks
as weird as shit anyway, and they were all saying, 'Who
are these weird people? This blonde and this other tall
skinny jerk and this little twerp, what IS GOING ON?'
Anyway, like fifty people wanted to get off the plane.

"The plane was held up, the captain was
grounded on the spot for opening the doors again in the
first place. We were still at the loading bay, but I honestly
don't remember if the engines were on or not. We weren't
moving.

"So we got off and Phil got off and I understand
that a lot of other people got off. The flight was delayed,
and they had to get another captain to take over.

"They took our luggage off, we waited for it,
and when it came we ran right over to get on the next
flight, and they took our luggage and sent it on through.
Phil was nowhere to be seen.

"Then just as we came away from getting our
tickets restamped, the guy came over to me and Ellie and
said, 'We don't really think we want you flying.' I said
what are you talking about? He said, 'Well, you disrupted
this whole flight, you and the other guy.' I said what other
guy? 'That little guy—he's not with you?' I said no, we

didn't know what was going on. Somebody was getting off the plane, and my wife's very blah blah blah. And besides, I said, our luggage is on the next flight and we're going to have to go through the whole thing again with the next flight.

"He said okay, and then Phil comes staggering down, and the word went from one airline to the next, not to let this guy on. He could not get out of Los Angeles—he had to go to another airport someplace else, where the word hadn't gotten yet.

"Ellie and I got on the other plane, and the guy comes round and says, 'Get off the plane.' So we got off and stood beside it—you know, where nobody ever goes? Where the guys with the earphones are? Right next to the big jet. And there's our luggage. 'Open it,' they said. It was a bomb scare . . . they figured maybe these weirdos were bombers. Everybody in the plane is looking out at us, and we're running through the luggage and showing them that there's no bomb.

"It was okay, so we put it back and closed it up and got back on. People were . . . *looking* at us."

As recently as October, 1971, when Phil was visiting John and Yoko's art exhibition in Syracuse, New York, he reportedly refused to board the plane on the way back for fear of it crashing. He had tried to persuade Ringo Starr to take another flight with him, but eventually went alone on a separate plane.

"He probably wasn't getting enough attention," commented Barry of the incident. "He would know all the time what he was doing. I'm sure he believes that he's too divine ever to crash."

᠅

One of the less publicized facets of Spector's career in the Philles days is his association with Lenny

Bruce, the great comedian who was persecuted throughout his career by the law, and died a junkie in Hollywood in August, 1966.

Danny Davis knew Bruce before Spector did: "I knew Lenny in New York, when he was doing light humor. He used to hang out at Hansen's Drug Store, at the corner of 51st and 7th Avenue. He was known as one of Hansen's Boys, because that's where he took his calls and met his agents and so on.

"When he came out to California, and Phil latched onto him, Lenny was amazed to see me there. To tell you the truth, Phil was a bit of a Johnny-come-lately there; Phil only really got into him in his last days. He put out an album by Lenny on Philles, with the famous cover picture of Lenny sitting on a john in a graveyard. It didn't sell much; Lenny wasn't yet a cult, he hadn't made the grade then. Phil put Lenny into a theatre in Hollywood, on LaBrea, and took a tremendous beating. Lenny had asked him to sponsor a one-man show, but it was in Lenny's last days and it was tragic. He wasn't funny at all.

"When Lenny killed himself, Phil and I went up to see the body laid out in Lenny's home. It was one of the most unsavory nights of my life. Going back, Phil took the wheel of the Cadillac and went down the canyon looking in the air and carrying on. . . . I don't know whether it was genuine grief or just for show, but I was positive that we'd go over a cliff-edge before we got back to Sunset Boulevard.

"Now I've never told this to anyone before, but after Lenny died, the police took pictures of him lying there, with the needle still in his arm. Not many days after that, a Los Angeles detective came round and asked if I wanted to buy pictures of Lenny in the death pose. It was amazing, and I asked him why? What would we do with them? 'Put them on an album cover,' he said. I told him to go away.

"Later, I told Phil about the guy coming round with the pictures, and that I'd said we didn't want them. Well, you could have heard the scream over in London. He insisted that I call back straight away and bought them. And he paid *five thousand dollars* for those negatives, from the Los Angeles Police Department. To me, it was just the most amazing thing in the world."

Maybe he bought them to stop them from getting into anybody else's hands and being used in an unscrupulous way?

"There was a time when I wanted to believe that. I guess I still try to cling to it."

❧

Almost all of Spector's Philles artists made many more records for him than those already mentioned, of course.

THE CRYSTALS

The original quintet lost one member in their first year of existence, 1962, when Mary left to get married. That brought them down to a permanent unit of lead singer Lala Brooks, plus Barbara Alston, Dee Dee Kennibrew, and Pat Wright. The only subsequent change came in October, 1963, when Pat left to get married and was replaced by Frances Collins, who first appeared with the group on a tour of Britain in February '64.

The group's success tapered off very fast after "Then He Kissed Me," probably because Phil was more interested in the potential of the Ronettes, whose sound was better suited to the approach he had developed.

But the Crystals made several fine records which weren't as successful as they deserved to be. The follow-up to "Then He Kissed Me"—"Little Boy"—although not a classic is notable for the way Lala's voice mixes into the track: it seems more like another string line than a lead line. And the track itself is dynamite, rumbling and thundering like an approaching storm.

"Little Boy" only just crept inside the Hot 100. Spector quickly cut another record with them, "I Wonder." A much better song, it was never issued in the States, but appeared in England just in time for their February tour—with "Little Boy" on the flip. "I Wonder" is tremendous (much better than the Ronettes' album cut on the same song), with tambourines and violins flying all over the place and earthquake explosions from Hal Blaine's drums. It possesses a sheer velocity which Spector rarely equalled, and certainly didn't deserve its ignominious fate.

The Crystals' final throw was "All Grown Up," their fifth consecutive Spector/Barry/Greenwich song. Based on a Chuck Berry number called "Almost Grown," it showed a strong Berry/R & B influence. The sound was much more raw than their usual records, with flat rock and roll guitar and Morse Code piano, and the backup "baa-doo-day," was a direct development from Berry's song. Again, lots of energy—and again, failure. It hit number 98 in the chart, and that was the last to be heard of the Crystals for a long, long time.

Philles released three Crystals albums—*Twist Uptown, He's A Rebel,* and *The Crystals Sing The Greatest Hits, Volume One*—there was no Volume Two—but they were, pardon the expression, a real con. Four of the tracks appeared on all three albums. The only difference between *Twist Uptown* and *He's A Rebel* is that they took the former, axed two tracks and added three more, and put it out as the latter. The albums were simply intended to be, in Spector's own immortal phrase, "two hit songs and ten pieces of junk."

The *Greatest Hits* album consisted mostly of other people's greatest hits: "The Twist," the Dartells' "Hot Pastrami," the Orlons' "Wah-Watusi," and Dee Dee Sharp's "Mashed Potato Time." It was obviously thrown together in a great hurry. The best track, apart from their own hits, is a very sweet rendering of Richard Barrett's "Look In My Eyes," a hit for the Chantels (Carlton 555) in '61. At least some care was devoted to the string writing here, and it came out much less perfunctory than the others. On "Hot Pastrami," the girls sing the names of Spector and Jack Nitzsche—and it's possible to detect Bobby Sheen's voice in the background.

After "All Grown Up," the group parted company with Spector and went to United Artists, where they made two fairly dire singles: "My Place" backed with "You Can't Tie A Good Girl Down" (927) and "Are You Trying to Get Rid Of Me, Baby?" backed with "I Got A Man" (994). They were forced into a sub-Vandellas groove, and chart action was not forthcoming.

So the Crystals went off to become housewives. They did not appear again until mid-1971, when they popped up, looking prettier and *much* sexier, on one of Richard Nader's Rock And Roll Revival concerts.

Still, to Barbara Alston and Lala Brooks, a big "thank you."

THE RONETTES

Phil fell in love with Ronnie almost as soon as he saw her, and the records they made together reflect that feeling between them. There almost seems to be an extra-special warmth in the tracks he created to surround her extraordinary voice.

Brian Wilson reckons that the Ronettes' "Be My Baby" is the best record of all time—but their follow-up, "Baby I Love You," can't be far behind. Though the way Ronnie warbles "oo-wee-baby" is indescribable, the song only went to number 24, and the next one, "(The Best Part Of) Breakin' Up," did no better than 39. The first song Phil wrote with Anders and Poncia, it boasts one of the best false endings ever made. The background vocals on "Breakin' Up"—especially the way they mingle with the lead—may also be the finest Phil ever wrote.

The fourth single, "Do I Love You," was written by the same team, but it's disappointing. Nice, certainly, even pleasantly mellow—but lacking the energy to make it click. The mix is odd, too, with the horns sticking out unpleasantly.

"Do I Love You" was followed by two monsters, probably the best records the group ever made. "Walking In The Rain" has such a lovely lyric idea for a start. Barry and Cynthia came up with words: the girl says she'll know Mr. Right when he comes along because he'll enjoy the same things that she does—"like walking in the rain. . . ." Such a simple, lovely thought, and it's couched in a tune and arrangement which are genuinely delicate.

"Walkin' In The Rain" reversed their fortunes slightly. For the Ronettes' next outing, Phil tried out another collaboration with Mann and Weil called "Born To Be Together." This one sounds almost supernatural, with epic violin glissandi and thudding, indistinct drums. It brings to mind another Spector saying: "I don't believe in eight tracks and sixteen tracks. . . . I like to record on one track in monaural. The biggest records I've ever made were all done on one track. To me, the cloudier and fuzzier a record is, the more honesty and guts it has." "Born To Be Together" proves that belief a thousand times over.

The last real Ronettes record was intended to be a Spector song called "Oh I Love You." The song wasn't anything very special, so the DJ's flipped it and found on the B side a rare Spector/King/Goffin song called "Is

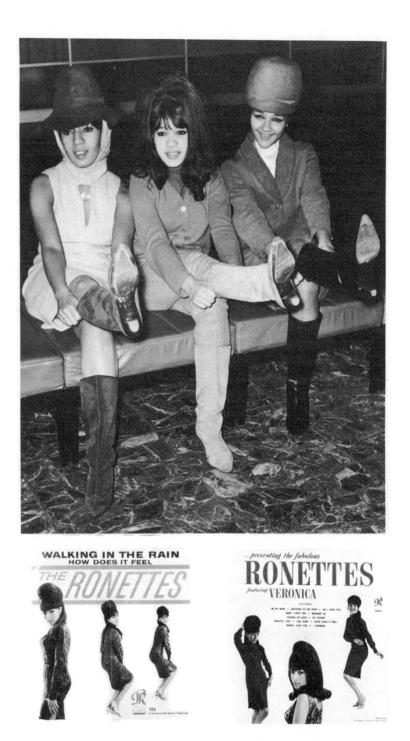

This What I Get For Loving You?'". It was a little noisier than the intended A side and slightly more distinguished. The jockeys played it quite a lot, and it climbed to number 75.

The absolute last Ronettes' record for Philles came toward the end of the label's life. Phil was so dispirited that he gave the group over to Jeff Barry, who cut "I Can Hear Music" with them. It was okay and that was all; the Beach Boys later did it much better on Capitol.

Meanwhile, the group's biggest hits had already been collected on an album called *Presenting The Fabulous Ronettes*—which, for once, was very good value. Apart from the five singles, there was a cut entitled "So Young" by one P. Tyus, a song Phil had apparently tried to put out as a Veronica single on one of his subsidiary labels, with no response from the public. The Beach Boys later did this one too on their *Beach Boys Today* album (Brian Wilson also recorded his own versions of two Crystals songs, "There's No Other" and "Then He Missed Me." A true fan.) The album also included the Ronettes' version of "I Wonder," probably recorded before the Crystals' rendition of the same song because it is much less ambitious and flamboyant. There are two further beauties: the super-romantic "You Baby," in the adoring tradition of their early singles, and a lovely Spector ballad called "When I Saw You," a solo for Ronnie over a D—B-minor—G—A version of the "Earth Angel" progression. They take it at a funereal pace. As she sings it you can almost see Ronnie staring over the mike and through the glass partition into Phil's eyes. It was later put out as the flip side of "I Can Hear Music."

The only downers are "Chapel of Love," which Jeff Barry recorded with the Dixie Cups (Red Bird 10-001) for a number one hit; a live version of "What'd I Say," which breaks the mood; and a fast Spector/Anders/Poncia thing called "How Does It Feel?" which is fairly meaningless.

But they made some great records, didn't they? And Phil, the producer, married Ronnie, the leading lady, which is how all good movies end.

BOB B. SOXX/DARLENE LOVE

It is impossible to discuss these artists' work separately, because in effect they were interchangeable. They were the mainstays of a pool of singers which Phil permutated to suit his musical whims—sometimes their records were even issued under more than one name. For example, a cut called "My Heart Beat A Little Bit Faster" appeared on the Bob B. Soxx album, and later came out as a Darlene Love flip side, credited to Darlene—who actually did sing it.

The follow-up to Bob B. Soxx's "Zip-A-Dee-Doo-Dah" was a great track called "Why Do Lovers Break Each Other's Heart?", written by Phil and Ellie Greenwich with Tony Powers, a writer with Ellie before she met Jeff, and then a staff writer at Screen Gems. Sheen takes the "Mr. Bassman" intro, Darlene takes the lead. It really catches fire on the last chorus: after the piano break, when everybody suddenly starts clapping on the backbeat. Touches like that made the fans swing the needle right back to the beginning—and probably made them buy the record in the first place.

The follow-up was the furious but empty "Not Too Young To Get Married." Its saving grace is that it is strongly reminiscent of the U.S. Bonds records, particularly in the tenor riffs. A good party record, and the Blue Jeans' last single.

The first two singles were also included on the Bob

B. Soxx *Zip-A-Dee-Doo-Dah* album, which is notable if only for the fact that it must be one of the only pop albums that gives no indication whatsoever of the titles anywhere on the sleeve—just a paragraph of hype from the producer and a list of musicians' credits. There were some real dogs on this album: "This Land Is Your Land," "White Cliffs Of Dover," "Let The Good Times Roll" . . . all pretty bad.

But the compensation was there, and makes it worth looking for today. First, there was a "novelty rhythm" tune by Spector called "Dear (Here Comes My Baby)," featuring Sheen on an updated Coasters type song, with positively superb vocal harmony. An insane little track, it is full of seemingly irrelevant, clattering percussion—real charming.

Even odder was "Everything's Gonna Be Alright," a straight blues sung by Sheen, double tracked, in a mushmouth Jimmy Reed style. Sheen is backed by two booming electric basses, a distant snare drum and tenor sax, desultory vocalists, and a guitar solo where the guitar player sounds as if he only met the instrument a few minute before. It is probably one of the worst guitar solos ever recorded. Amazingly, another take of the backing track alone later surfaced as the B side of Darlene's "Christmas" single, under the title "Harry and Milt Meet Hal B." . . . with an equally bad guitar solo.

The Bob B. Soxx album also includes a very good Spector song called "Baby (I Love You)"—not the Ronettes' song. No prizes for guessing the chord progression. That's right: C—A minor—F—G. Its overall sound is a dead ringer for Rosie and the Originals' "Angel Baby," and might just have been considered for a single. Darlene leads the excellent girl-group vocal.

Finally, on this curate's egg of a record, are two compositions by Jackie DeShannon and Sharon Sheeley—Jimmy Baby," about a returning soldier, right in the Shirelles' tradition, and "I Shook The World." Both are good, like much of this album—an album intended as a cynical hotch-potch, which turned out anything but.

Darlene's first solo single was also her best: "(Today I Met) The Boy I'm Gonna Marry," an excellent Spector/Greenwich/Powers song given a strong, stately treatment. Darlene really puts herself into it—and it should have done better than 39th on the chart.

Her second record has more renown, but is not as good. "Wait Til My Bobby Gets Home," a very chirpy record along the emotional lines of the Angels' great "My Boyfriend's Back," saw Powers replaced in the writing team by Ellie's new soulmate, Jeff Barry. It was a more commercial record, and the same writing combination produced her third hit, the surging "A Fine, Fine Boy," with its amazing finale: as the orchestra banks down, Darlene yells: "My boy . . . he's a fine, fine, *superfine* boy." It was her last chart entry.

However, twice, in the Decembers of '63 and '64, Spector issued her best track from the Christmas album, "Christmas (Baby Please Come Home)" as a potential seasonal hit. The first time, it had the "Harry And Milt Meet Hal B." flipside; in '64, this was replaced by another Christmas track, "Winter Wonderland." On neither occasion did it warm many Yuletide hearths.

It is a shame that Darlene did not do better as a soloist—she had a tremendous voice with a zestful attack. After she had peaked with Philles, she returned to singing backgrounds with the Blossoms. Tony Hall recalls visiting Phil in Hollywood some years ago and seeing, lying on a desk, a pile of unissued Darlene Love masters. "Any normal girl singer would have given an arm for those masters," he remarks.

And Bobby Sheen? He went the same route. His name appeared once on a Capitol single around 1966, called "Doctor Love." He sounded rather like Major Lance—it was very good indeed. Phil always could pick them.

ALLEY CATS

Back in '62, Lou Adler handled Kirshner's West Coast business in the Hollywood office of Aldon Music. He and Phil remembered each other from the Teddy Bear days, and built up a good working relationship.

Adler was in business with Herb Alpert, managing groups. One of them, a black quartet from Los Angeles called the Alley Cats, had been previously known either as the Valiants and the Untouchables. Their lead singer, Billy Storm, had already made some records for Columbia, and the rest of the group consisted of Chester Pipkin, Ed Wallis, and Bryce Caufield, who'd cut for Madison. Adler took them to Phil's office one day, and Spector liked them enough to cut one record with them.

It was a Caufield/Pipkin/Willis song called "Puddin' N' Tain (Ask Me Again, I'll Tell You The Same)." It too fell into the "novelty rhythm" category, being based on the old kids' rhyme. Adler himself produced the B side, Caufield and Pipkin's very ordinary "Feel So Good" (so Jeff Barry is not quite "the only living person who ever produced a record on Phil's label," as he claims).

"Puddin N' Tain" is fast and bouncy, taking its bass-drum orientation from the Monotones' old "Book Of Love" hit. Storm sings a very good falsetto lead. Like Bob B. Soxx's "Dear," it's an excellent example of how Spector could take an antique style and make something both personal and slightly humorous out of it. The record didn't do badly, but it was the only record the Alley Cats ever made for Phil . . . or almost.

He later used some of them as background voices on the Checkmates' A & M album. But by that time, they were known as Africa, and Caufield had made more solo records, this time for Omen.

Adler's final word on the group: "Chester Pipkin is now making commercials with black groups, and the other guys are like . . . uh . . . mailmen. I see them every once in a while."

RIGHTEOUS BROTHERS

How on earth can you follow the best record ever made? The answer is that you can't, even if your name is Spector. The second Righteous Brothers single on Philles, "Just Once In My Life," had been written by Phil with Carole King and Gerry Goffin. It wasn't really worthy of its illustrious predecessor—the beauiful quiet section came much too late in the record, and the hook phrase wasn't so hot either.

Their next one, however, was a return to solid dynamite: a new arrangement of the standard "Unchained Melody." (Remember the first Teddy Bears album?) Hatfield is featured on this one. He starts out over soft arpeggios, maraccas accentuating the 12/8 time ever so quietly. For 32 bars, the song remains very attractive but slightly subdued. Then, on the first beat of the second chorus, Earl Palmer's crash cymbal smashes the quietness and shifts the mood into something more urgent. Hatfield responds—listen to the way he sings that second, melismatic "hunger"—and strings and voices build up in the background. The piece stays controlled though, never quite destroying itself, and ends with a fulsome *rallentando*.

Its B side featured another Spector/King/Goffin song called "Hung On You," a tune which might logically have been expected to be the top deck, since it contained many of the elements of the first two singles. It is much better than "Just Once In My Life," for it presents Medley at his harshest and most urgent. God only knows how many singers there are in the background choir, but the session fees must have totaled a small fortune.

Never one to miss the chance of making a "formula" record, Spector duly noted the success of "Unchained Melody," and the duet's last two singles on Philles were both standard songs, blown up to Cinemascope. "Ebb Tide," arranged by Perry Botkin, Jr., reached fifth on the chart, but the subsequent "The White Cliffs of Dover," arranged by Gene Page, did nothing at all, probably because Spector had lost interest by then.

These last Righteous Brothers records seem somehow to subvert the original concept behind "Lovin' Feelin'," which may have been a big production, but it was still great rock and roll—and it appealed to 16 year olds. "Ebb Tide" was *older* music, it had nothing for kids to relate to. In retrospect it almost looks like a plot to aim the Brothers straight into the heart of Las Vegas.

The Righteous Brothers' three Philles albums, *You've Lost That Lovin' Feelin'*, *Just Once In My Life*, and *Back to Back*, were useless if you had already bought their singles, because those singles were all Phil ever produced with them. He padded the albums out with Medley-produced versions of things like "Oo-Poo-Pah-Doo" and "Sticks And Stones," accompanied by something called The Mike Patterson Band. It was substandard, even for fans of their Moonglow records.

Right after "Ebb Tide," the Brothers quit Philles—because, says Danny Davis, they were sick of everybody talking about their records as Phil Spector creations, and not as Righteous Brothers hits. They went to MGM/Verve, where they started out very well. They cut a fine Mann/Weil song called "(You're My) Soul And Inspiration," released it on Verve 10383 on February 26, 1966, and it tore up to number one. They couldn't follow it up, though. The next record, "He," was number 18. The one after was 30 and the one after that was 47. Eventually they split up to go solo, but that didn't work out well either. Hatfield found another "brother" and reformed the duo, while Medley eventually landed a contract with A & M in '71, sang on a "rock cantata" called *Wings*, by the Frenchman, Michel Colombier, and was last seen planning a new solo album for A & M again, with Colombier arranging.

TODAY'S HITS

Today's Hits was the title of an album Spector put out in the Autumn of '63 which showcased some of his biggest early hits with Philles. Curiosities abound, though: the Crystals were represented not only by "Da Doo Ron Ron" and "Then He Kissed Me," but also by "Oh Yeah, Maybe Baby," the B side of their first single. Yesterday's flip side, today's hit?

Darlene Love had four tracks on the album: her first two A sides and "My Heart Beat A Little Bit Faster," the B side from "The Boy I'm Gonna Marry." But the fourth track was a Spector song called "Playing For Keeps," a lovely blues ballad which reminds me a little of Mable John's great "Your Real Good Thing" on Stax a few years later. As far as I can trace, "Playing For Keeps" never appeared on a 45 in America, but it did in Britain, as the B side of "The Boy I'm Gonna Marry."

The other tracks included the three Bob B. Soxx hits, the Alley Cats' record, and the Ronettes' "Be My Baby."

One more thing. . . . The liner note was penned by none other than Mrs. Annette Spector. It's a *genre* classic, a real collector's item.

She writes: "I wish that all of you could come to a Phil Spector recording session, and be able to meet him, and all of his wonderful artists, and see as I have, just how all the hits are born, and all of the time, effort and talent that is put into each recording, just for your enjoyment, created solely with you in mind, by the master of today's music—Phil Spector.

"By the way, the reason I know so much about Phil, is right after one session, we were married."

6

THE IKE AND TINA FIASCO
"I really liked it, anyway...."

THE FRONT PAGE OF *BILLBOARD* ON MAY 14, 1966, carried a two-column color picture of Ike and Tina Turner.

Beneath the picture ran a brief story in 6-pt. type: "Philles Records recently added the dynamic duo, Ike and Tina Turner, to their roster. The couple's first release, entitled 'River Deep—Mountain High,' was produced by Philles prexy Phil Spector. In addition, the Philles label acquired the Ikettes, whose release will be forthcoming soon. (Advertisement)"

The following week, a review put "River Deep" among the magazine's Top 60 Pick selections. The critique read: "Exciting dance beat production backs a wailin' Tina vocal on a solid rock tune penned by Barry and Greenwich."

One week later, on May 29, "River Deep" made its first entry into the *Billboard* Hot 100, at number 98.

On June 4, it was 94.

On June 11, it climbed a place to 93.

On June 18, it skipped five rungs to 88.

On June 25, it was out.

And it never came back.

For Philip Spector, it was the most appalling blow of his career—a sharp and vicious chop in the place where it hurt most: his ego.

Its consequences for him were sudden and violent.

He retired from the business completely, did not make another record for two years, and disappeared into the California desert, apparently finished.

❧

As pointed out before, Spector always preferred to work with black singers. Tina was a natural for him. The most uninhibited act in the business, she and Ike had been around for years, making great little records like "It's Gonna Work Out Fine" and "A Fool In Love" for the small labels, Sue and Kent. They had had a consistent impact on the R & B market—"Gonna Work Out Fine" (Sue 749) even got to number 14 in the national chart in 1961.

Throughout their career, Ike had Svengali'd Tina. A very tough, foxy guy, he had choreographed their act right down to the exact pitch of Tina's every wail and the last unison pelvic twitch from the Ikettes. But he never really understood how to get her across to the huge white audience of that era—the Ike and Tina Turner Revue was apparently condemned to the seven-nights-a-week haul around and across America on the R & B circuit.

Here though was Phil Spector, on a movie set in Los Angeles, conferring with Ike. The Turners had been called in as a replacement for the movie act, The T'N'T Show, because somebody had got sick. They were meeting Spector for the first time.

Phil's opening gambit was an offer to produce Tina. He'd just lost the Righteous Brothers, and the Ronettes weren't doing the business he would have liked. He needed something fast.

Tina was just right. A real professional and a good singer, she sounded like no one else—even though her previous records had been poorly produced. She was a jewel in search of a setting, and here was Phil Spector, the world's hottest producer, offering to put her up there with the biggest. According to Bud Dain, then general manager of Liberty Records, Spector was giving Ike "an absolute guarantee of hits forever." (1)

Ike didn't have to think very hard about the offer. He had just switched labels from Loma, Warner Brothers' R & B subsidiary, to Kent, and he wasn't happy about the way it was working out. When Spector offered 20,000 dollars in front, Ike grabbed and held on tight.

That 20,000 dollars payment, it transpired, was conditional on Ike's having absolutely nothing to do with the recordings. In fact Spector told him that he should not even attend the sessions. In his usual way, Spector wanted full control over every note Tina sang. He knew that Ike had bossed all his wife's previous records—this time Ike could stay home and mind the kids.

The next job was to write a song for her. Phil called up Jeff Barry and Ellie Greenwich, and they got together to work on something special.

Spector remembers it thus: "It was the first thing I had written with Jeff and Ellie since the early hits. I hadn't seen them for a couple of years and, in the meantime, they'd divorced. When I got together with them again I didn't know they were divorced. . . . Every time we'd

Although Ike Turner appeared with Tina and Spector in this picture on the back of the original "River Deep—Mountain High" album sleeve, Spector insisted that he should not attend the sessions. Which perhaps explains his expression.

write a love line, Ellie would start to cry. I couldn't figure out what was happening, and then I realized . . . it was a very uncomfortable situation. We wrote that, and we wrote 'I Can Hear Music'. . . . We wrote three or four hit songs on that one writing session.

"The whole thing about 'River Deep' was the way I could feel that strong bass line. That's how it started. And then Jeff came up with the opening line. I wanted a tender song about a chick who loved somebody very much, but a different way of expressing it. So we came up with the rag doll and 'I'm going to cuddle you like a little puppy.' And the idea was really built for Tina, just like 'Lovin' Feelin'' was built for the Righteous Brothers." (2)

The writing session took a couple of weeks, and then Phil started laying down the rhythm tracks, using

Nitzsche to arrange once again. It was the biggest production he ever made, in every way.

"That record was to be his crowning achievement," says Danny Davis. "When I left the company, the bills on that one single side came to 22,000 dollars, and I don't believe they were all in then. He'd spent so much time on mixing and dubbing, going back time and again to put on something he'd just thought of. That amount of money would be outrageous for an album today, never mind a single in 1966."

Finally, on the night of March 7, Tina arrived at Gold Star to add the vocal track.

"Tina's voice was really polished," says Spector. "She reminded me of a female Ben E. King, and of the old days. I knew she'd be able to sing it great."

How can one describe the A side of Philles 131? It begins with those thunderous basses and tympani playing a sharply stepped intro, then it crashes to a halt and in comes Tina: "When I was a little girl I had a rag doll the only doll I've ever owned. Now I love you just the way I loved that rag doll . . . but only now that love has grown."

Immediately, the listener is thrown into a crazy melange of emotions. This heavy thighed Earth Mother, wailing like there's a hellhound on her trail, is singing about rag dolls and puppies. It sounds silly, but it comes out just right.

But the *SOUND*. . . . God, what sound. Mountains, walls, valleys, caverns, chasms, cliffs—a world full of noise, it seems, only channeled into something approaching that "rushing, mighty wind" the Bible talks about.

Spector had tried to make it the biggest, thickest sound that any man had ever created, and he succeeded. It's really almost impossible to pick out the individual instruments: the drums merge into the basses, which merge into the guitars, which merge into the strings, which merge into the voices, which merge into . . . some inaudible astral frequency.

And on top of it all there's Tina, every molecule of her body straining for that last great cosmic scream.

At the end comes one giant thump, then a vast silence. You knew the first time you heard it that the world would never be quite the same place again.

Ȝ

How could it possibly fail? Many plausible explanations have been offered; the truth seems to be a combination of all of them.

First, Spector himself: "People just didn't care for it, the disk jockeys wouldn't play it." Too simple, Phil. Was there an element of jealousy involved? "It reached the point of antagonism, where people said 'Who does he think he is? He never takes us to dinner' . . . things like that. Resentment built up. I thought the record was good. I really liked it, anyway."

Second, Ike Turner: "See, what's wrong with America, I think, is that rather than accept something for its value . . . what it's doing, America mixes Race in it. You can't call that record R & B. But because it's Tina . . . if you had not put Tina's name on there and put 'Joe Blow,' then the Top 40 stations would have accepted it for being a pop record. But Tina Turner . . . they want to brand her as being an R & B artist. I think the main reason that 'River Deep' didn't make it here in America was that the R & B stations wouldn't play it because they thought it was pop, and the pop stations wouldn't play it because they thought it was R & B. And it didn't get played at all. The only record I've heard that could come close to that record is a record by the Beach Boys called 'Good Vibrations.' I think these are the two records that I've heard in my life that I really like, you know?" (3)

Third, Jeff Barry: "When someone's on top, or let's say has a good reputation—and certainly Phil at that time was in that category—although it's never spoken of, I think that the industry as an animal, its single emotion is not one of good wishes, okay? You never hear a rumor like, 'Wow . . . Phil Spector is this' or 'Jeff Barry just bought a great car' or 'He just cut a great record.' You're most likely to hear 'Did you know Jeff Barry's fighting with Dusty Springfield?' So with the slightest ammunition, the industry as a whole is very quick to say that someone has had it. Phil being of his own sarcastic nature . . . and he has a self-destructive thing going for him, which is part of the reason that the mix on 'River Deep' is terrible, he buried the lead and he knows he buried the lead and he *cannot stop* himself from doing that . . . if you listen to his records in sequence, the lead goes further and further in and to me what he is saying is, 'It is *not* the song I wrote with Jeff and Ellie, it is *not* the song—just listen to those *strings*. I want *more* musicians, it's *me*, listen to that bass sound. . . .' That, to me, is what hurts in the long run. And at that time, as I recall it, he had said something about a disk jockey, made some kind of a comment about the radio station level, something like that, which spread like wildfire. So the stations and the industry as a whole, when they heard about it . . . you see they have a very negative attitude all the time, an attitude of 'Oh yeah? Let's see what you've come up with here . . . what is *that*? I can't hear that. That's an ego record . . . I can't hear the *song*.' They look for any reason, I think. Also, I do think that the song is not as clear on the record as it should be, mix-wise. I don't want to use the word overproduced, because it isn't, it's just undermixed. I think those two elements were enough for that record. He took that as a personal insult and subsequently ceased production, so we'll never know if the next record he might have made would have been a hit or not. The industry might have felt that it had taken its revenge, and made the next record a hit."

Fourth, Danny Davis: "It came at a time when a lot of people were finding fault with the overpowering backgrounds he liked to insert. Ike and Tina weren't thought of very highly at that time, either . . . they were thought of as an R & B act, and there was no way they could cross the line to Top 40. The record was also too long, at a time when long records weren't popular with the stations. A lot of the programmers felt that there was some stuff on 'River Deep' that was extraneous—and when Phil heard that they wanted to do major surgery on something he'd given his lifeblood to. . . ."

Fifth, Paul Case: "He was having some problems. The disk jockeys were making very big demands on him. They wanted personal appearances, and they wanted him to go on talk shows for interviews, and by nature this was something he didn't want to do unless the show was very important. He felt he didn't want to have to do them all, and I think that way he hurt himself a little with the disk jockeys. I think it was the manner in which he rejected the shows. I'm quite sure it had a bearing [on 'River Deep']."

The sixth point of view, from a close friend of Phil, was that Spector was blacklisted because he refused to pay the DJ's to play his records. This is only the personal feeling of that friend, thought it stands up well in terms of Phil's pride. At point he was too proud, too full of his own ego to feel that he had to press dollar bills into a disk jockey's hand just to get his records heard. As the anonymous friend said: "He thought that everybody should be waiting and anticipating eagerly when Phil Spector's name was on the logo as producer. This is what happened after the first few Crystals records—everybody was looking for the Phil Spector concept, the Phil Spector name on it, and it was getting played."

It was a hit in Britain though, reaching number 2 in some charts, and 3 in others by the middle of July. For any British kid even half way into pop music by 1966, it still stands as a landmark.

The reason for that maverick success in England was mainly Tony Hall, the Decca promotion man who had been partly responsible for the Philles/Decca tie-up in the first place.

"I believed in him like mad," says Hall, "and when I heard that record I phoned him and told him that I was going to try my damnedest for him." So Hall wrote individually to every radio disk jockey in Britain, pleading with them to play the record. He concentrated particularly on the pirate stations, now outlawed but then on based on offshore ships and disused oil rigs, which were wildly popular among young listeners dissatisfied with the staid policy of the BBC.

"I rallied round all the pirates," Hall remembers, "even though I wasn't officially supposd to have anything to do with them, because they were illegal. They all thought it was a great record, but an uncommercial one, but they said they'd help me. So it was the pirates who started it, and after the demand had grown, the BBC took it up."

Spector was quoted about its British success: "We can only assume that England is more appreciative of talent and exciting music than the U.S." And Ike Turner followed up with: "In England, they don't judge records according to Race or anything like that. They judge records on just what's on the record . . . and that's the way it should be."

❧

Around the same time that "River Deep" was cut, Spector also recorded several more songs with Tina. First was the B side of the single, a Spector-written up-tempo blues called "I'll Keep You Happy," a hard and driving number but basically just another throwaway so that no DJ could turn the record over.

In England, the follow-up to "River Deep" was a Spectorized treatment of the old Martha and the Vandellas B side, "A Love Like Yours (Don't Come Knocking Every Day)," written by Eddie and Brian Holland and Lamont Dozier. Tina's version is amazing: it sounds as if it were recorded in a cathedral, with massed strings and tom-toms frequently giving way to an almost sepulchral hush—which Tina fills with lung-bursting sound. Sometimes Spector makes his orchestra sound like one big guitar; here it sounds like a giant Welsh harp. The finale also displays the best crash cymbal ever committed to tape.

The B side of the English single (London HLU 10083) was a Barry/Greenwich song called "Hold On Baby," which had the same groundswell feeling as "River Deep." It was just as fast, but coarser and less distinguished: it comes across as a duet for voice and drums, separated by a mass of undifferentiated noise.

One year later, Spector's third Ike and Tina single was released in Britain: "I'll Never Need More Than This." Jeff Barry calls this the "sister song" to "River Deep," because they were written within a few weeks of each other for the same artist, and they have basically the same feeling.

There are times when I prefer this one to "River Deep," because of its longer, more elegant line, which still does not lose any of the explosive energy. Once again, the orchestra builds to a peak which bursts the heavens—like an aural reproduction of the universe constantly expanding. No Spector record has ever swung harder than this. Here the cymbal crashes, courtesy of Earl Palmer, expand like some giant mushroom cloud and hang over the entire production.

All these extra tracks were projected as future American singles and were even given catalogue numbers, but Spector abandoned them when the first one failed. Two tracks called "A Man Is a Man Is a Man" and "Two to Tango" were to have formed the first American follow-up, Philles 134, but they seem never to have seen the light of day. "I'll Never Need More Than This" was to be Philles 135, backed by something called "The Cashbox Blues," while "A Love Like Yours" was given number 136, with an Ike Turner production of "I Idolize You" on the B side.

A *River Deep–Mountain High* album first appeared in Britain in 1966, as London HAU 8298. It included two further Spector productions: a rolling "Save The Last Dance For Me," which had been the British B side of "I'll Never Need More Than This," and a fantastically powerful cut of Arthur Alexander's composition "Every Day I Have To Cry," originally Steve Alaimo's hit in 1963.

Unfortunately, the rest of the album was padded out with new Turner productions of old material: "It's Gonna Work Out Fine," "I Idolize You," "A Fool In Love," "Make 'Em Wait," "Oh Baby! (Things Ain't What They Used To Be)," "Such A Fool For You," and "You're So Fine"—all rather sadly reminiscent of Bill Medley's "productions" for the Righteous Brothers albums. At least the album featured some interesting cover shots: on the front was a Dennis Hopper collage, of which Bob Krasnow, then A & R man with Loma, says: "He was broke on his ass in Hollywood and trying photography. He took us to this sign company, where there was this 70-foot-high sign for a movie, with one of those sex stars—*Boccaccio '70* or something. And he shot them in front of that big teardrop. Then the gas company had a big sign, and Hopper took them there and shot them in front of a big burner." (4) On the back, there's a picture of Spector, flanked by Ike and Tina, leaning over the board at Gold Star.

*

"That record really put Phil out of business," says Danny Davis. "He took it as a deep personal insult, and it was a great personal tragedy for him. In fact I can't impress on you too greatly what a tragedy the whole thing was."

The worst thing, according to Davis, was for Spector to have to walk into Martoni's and not be acknowledged as the reigning king. Davis' subsequent experience reflects what must have been the prevalent mood around 9130 Sunset Boulevard in mid-1966.

"His recording schedule went dry, and he got a little sour. I was getting 800 dollars a week, but I'd go into the office every morning and there'd be nothing to promote, no records. Instead, there'd be a list on my desk, from Phil, of maybe fifteen things to do that morning."

The list would go something like this:

"1. Call the garage to have my mother's car serviced.

2. Call Minnesota Fats and see if he wants to shoot pool at my home this weekend.

3. Call Shelby and see if they can get four new tires for my car."

Et cetera, et cetera.

"Never anything to do with records. Now my forte is talking to disk jockeys, doing public relations. I had nothing to promote, so I told Phil: 'Look, I'm not a creative talent like you. If you don't let me do promotion, the next thing people will be asking is 'Danny Who?' So he'd give me another hundred dollars a week. Every time I said something, he'd give me another hundred. That's how he kept me. Finally, because I'd like to believe that I'm more of a man than that, I went and told him I was quitting. He never suspected that I'd actually do it and he countered by suing me for a quarter of a million dollars, because I still had four months to run on my contract with him."

By this time, Phil was getting involved in movies. He had agreed to finance Dennis Hopper's production of a film called *The Last Movie*. Davis says: "He was really into it. . . . Dennis had already scouted locations in Mexico, and he'd talked to studios. Suddenly Phil backed out, and they countered by suing him for 300,000 dollars. He needed my testimony, but when they called me I refused to give it unless he dropped his case against me. He did, I testified for him, and he won."

Hopper came back though to make the record-shattering and Establishment-wrecking *Easy Rider*, in which a small part was played by . . . Phil Spector. Davis's interpretation of Spector's nonspeaking role as a dope dealer in the movie will certainly interest seekers after hidden messages:

"You know that bit where Phil's in the movie, where he just sniffs the coke and doesn't talk at all? That's Dennis's way of shutting Phil up. That's what the picture is saying . . . for Dennis, it was the supreme thing, to shut Phil up. It was kinda wild. And you know what? When Dennis came back, after making *Easy Rider* and it being such a success, out of all the buildings he could have picked in

Los Angeles, he chose to rent space in Phil's building on Sunset Strip. Phil grooved on that, though, and told all his friends about it."

And *The Last Movie*, apparently abandoned in chaos after Phil pulled out, was finally made in Peru in 1970, and released the following year.

❨

Philles was dying though, after a glorious five-year history which had set the music industry on its ear. Phil had patently lost interest. Only two records were released after the "River Deep" fiasco (he had already give the Turners away to another producer, Bob Crewe).

One was the Righteous Brothers' "The White Cliffs Of Dover" backed with "She's Mine, All Mine." That was simply scraping the barrel, since both had been on the *Back To Back* album. The other was a Ronettes' single, "I Can Hear Music," backed with "When I Saw You." "I Can Hear Music" made the absolute bottom rung of the Billboard Hot 100 on October 29, 1966.

After that it was all over. Finished. The King was dead, and nobody bothered to wave goodbye.

7

OPENING THE DOOR

BY THE TIME PHIL QUIT IN '66 HE HAD LEFT AN indelible mark on the pop music world. Not only had he proved that youth could take charge, but he'd changed the whole sound and style of the music.

It's hard to assess his influence on any particular record—but most important is the general metamorphosis which he made possible.

First though, we must look at what went before. The last really important pop record to appear before Philles began was "Will You Love Me Tomorrow," the first big hit for the writing team of Carole King and Gerry Goffin. From Spector's point of view, it was important because it was the first real New York Girl Group record, the area in which he started off Philles with the Crystals.

"Will You Love Me Tomorrow" proved that girls could emulate what the Drifters had been doing for some years. Luther Dixon's arrangement for the Shirelles was extremely influential. In point of fact, the arrangement is probably as much Carole King's work as Dixon's—Tony Orlando, who sang the original demo of the song, has said that producers would often copy the way Carole treated her songs at the demo stage, simply because her ideas were always the right ones.

Dixon created a vocal sound at once girlish and wistful. It did not matter that lead singer Shirley Owens sometimes sang out of tune—it was the tone of her voice that mattered. Dixon surrounded her with a sweeping but basically simple string arrangement, violins playing behind the vocal what they would have played in the instrumental bridge of a Stoller arrangement for the Drifters.

Spector's work with the Crystals was the first real development of Dixon's achievement with the Shirelles. Spector beefed up the sound by adding his own production touches and using extra percussion techniques—probably derived from Bo Diddley's R & B records (which used maracas and tambourine), as well as the Drifters' Baion-style hits. Thus he took some of the load off the girl singers and gave more impetus to the backing—the girls now sounded even more passive.

The early Crystals records were almost certainly an influence on the Chiffons and their producer, Hank Medress. Medress was a member of the Tokens, and later the producer of Tony Orlando and Dawn. Medress brought the Chiffons up to the ultimate flowering of the NYGG style and held them there for a while, whereas Spector with the Crystals, and particularly with the Ronettes, went far beyond the restrictions of the basic approach. The Chiffons' "He's So Fine" and "One Fine Day" on Laurie are their best efforts; the latter in particular has a thick, churning sound which suggests the spiritual presence of Spector.

A favorite girl group record of many is the Angels' "My Boyfriend's Back," written and produced by the Feldman/Goldstein/Gottehrer team (who were members of the Strangeloves) for the Smash label. A lesser known classic is the Four Pennies' "When The Boy's Happy (The Girl's Happy Too)," a Barry/Greenwich song on Rust in 1963. The vocal treatment here is pure Chiffons, but the hammering piano can only have been suggested by Phil's early Los Angeles productions. It's an extraordinary record, which only improves with the passing years.

The finest tribute of all however, were paid to Spector through an entire label, Red Bird Records, set up by Leiber, Stoller, and George Goldner in 1964, with Jeff Barry and Ellie Greenwich as shareholders. According to Barry, the idea was to capitalize on all the writers and producers Leiber and Stoller had floating around. For a couple of years the label was an outstanding success, scoring huge hits by the Dixie Cups and the Shangri-Las in particular.

Red Bird was based around the girl group sound, even though it included other kind of artists (R & B singer Alvin Robinson, for instance). Spector's influence was paramount. You hear it strongly on an album called *Red Bird Goldies* (RB 20-102), which features all the above mentioned performers, plus the Butterflies, the Jelly Beans, the Ad Libs, and the Tradewinds (Anders and Poncia).

Jeff Barry produced most of the groups, including the Dixie Cups and, at the beginning, the Shangri-Las. The latter group was quickly taken over by a young iconoclast called George "Shadow" Morton, who put the motorbike noises on the famous "Leader Of The Pack" and, with Barry and Artie Ripp, was responsible for the seagulls-

and-surf effects on the group's first record, "Remember (Walking In The Sand)."

But it was Barry's production of the Jelly Beans' and the Butterflies' cuts that bore the strongest traces of Spector. It showed most overtly on the latter group's version of "I Wonder," the Spector/Barry/Greenwich song already recorded by the Crystals and the Ronettes. Barry does a great job of conjuring up the Philles atmosphere (the lead singer was a cross between Lala Brooks and Ronnie, which helped), but his treatment is much more obvious and predictable, with comparatively less energy. Barry's other Butterflies' record, "Goodnight Baby," was a beauty, though, as was the Jelly Beans' "Baby Be Mine," a classic of   subtle   seduction   with   a   smoky,   swirling

RB 20-102

Red Bird GOLDIES

SIDE ONE

1. CHAPEL OF LOVE—
THE DIXIE CUPS
Jeff Barry, Ellie Greenwich, Phil Spector
Trio Music Co., Inc. BMI
Produced by Leiber Stoller

2. REMEMBER (WALKING IN THE
SAND)—THE SHANGRI-LAS
George Morton—Trio Music Co. &
Tender Tunes Music, Inc. BMI
Produced by Jeff Barry & Artie Ripp
A Kama Sutra Production

3. NEW YORK'S A LONELY TOWN—
THE TRADE WINDS
Andreoli & Poncia, Jr.—Big Top, BMI
Produced by Anders Poncia

4. I WANNA LOVE HIM SO BAD—
THE JELLY BEANS
Jeff Barry & Ellie Greenwich
Trio Music Co., Inc. BMI
Produced by Jeff Barry & Steve Venet

5. GOOD NIGHT BABY—
THE BUTTERFLYS
Jeff Barry, Ellie Greenwich, Steve Venet
Trio Music Co., Inc. BMI
Produced by Jeff Barry & Steve Venet

6. GIVE HIM A GREAT BIG KISS—THE SHANGRI-LAS
George Morton—Trio Music Co. & Tender Tunes Music Inc. BMI
Produced by Shadow Morton
A Kama Sutra Production

SIDE TWO

1. LEADER OF THE PACK—
THE SHANGRI-LAS
Jeff Barry, Ellie Greenwich, George Morton
Trio Music Co., Inc. & Tender Tunes Music, In. BMI
Produced by Shadow Morton & Jeff Barry
A Kama Sutra Production

2. THE BOY FROM NEW YORK CITY—
THE AD LIBS
John Taylor, Trio Music Co., Inc. BMI
Produced by Leiber Stoller

3. SOMETHING YOU GOT—
ALVIN ROBINSON
Chris Kenner—Tune-Rel Publ., Inc. BMI
Produced by Leiber Stoller

4. I WONDER—THE BUTTERFLYS
Jeff Barry, Ellie Greenwich, Phil Spector
Trio Music Co., Inc. BMI
Produced by Jeff Barry & Steve Venet

5. BABY BE MINE—
THE JELLY BEANS
Jeff Barry, Ellie Greenwich, Steve Venet
Trio Music Co., Inc. BMI
Produced by Jeff Barry & Steve Venet

6. PEOPLE SAY—THE DIXIE CUPS
Jeff Barry, Ellie Greenwich
Trio Music Co., Inc. BMI
Produced by Leiber Stoller

*Courtesy Blue Cat Records Inc.

RED BIRD RECORDS-STUYVESANT PRODUCTIONS, INC., 1619 BROADWAY, NEW YORK, N.Y. 10019
1965 Stuyvesant Productions Inc. Printed in U.S.A.

atmosphere—rather like a Ronettes cut listened to through a cotton filter.

Unhappily, Red Bird folded in somewhat mysterious circumstances, leaving behind a legacy richer than most labels of ten times its size and longevity.

Again, it's hard to be specific, but certainly Spector exerted some influence on the Motown production teams. Motown cut loose musically in late '63, with records like Martha and the Vandellas' "Heatwave," and Mary Wells' "You Lost The Sweetest Boy"—veering away from their previous anonymity into a much more energetic form of production, with the emphasis on a dense, undifferentiated backing track and a superb snare drum sound. Spector's innovations paved the way for such a venture, the basis of Motown's considerable success over the decade.

More generally, it is difficult to imagine that the recent giant Diana Ross productions would have been possible, had not Spector pioneered enlarging the scope of recording. The same goes for the extravaganzas created by Isaac Hayes and Curtis Mayfield in the early part of the Seventies.

Spector's influence was not limited to black artists however. The surfing groups of 1963-65 came strongly under his spell, particularly Jan and Dean, whose hilariously ghoulish "Dead Man's Curve" and pretty "You Really Know How To Hurt A Guy" (both on Liberty) display unmistakably Spectoresque traits.

Brian Wilson's studio work with the Beach Boys was of course heavily motivated by Wilson's veneration of Spector. The Beach Boys' *Pet Sounds* album was a breakthrough in terms of studio rock largely instigated by Spector. Phil has been a major inspiration behind the advancements of recent years, and a pioneer of the freedom groups now possess in the studio.

The trend setting British groups of 1963 onwards were not touched by him greatly with the single important exception of the Rolling Stones. Their first producer, Andrew Loog Oldham, was trying to move the group from R & B into pop. His efforts in this sphere—"Tell Me" for instance—display more than a little of the techniques of Spector, whom he admired so much. That still doesn't make the Stones' early material into anything more than shoddy records which simply get worse as they get older.

As far as Britain goes, there's one more record to mention. Spector had been off the scene for more than a year when, in 1968, a record appeared on the English Parlophone label by a duo called Simon and Pi, "Sha La La Lee." Written by Kenny Lynch and Morty Shuman, the song had been a hit for the Small Faces a couple of years before, but for this outing it was masterminded by a young man named Mark Wirtz, notable for his composition of a "teenage opera" which was much ballyhooed, but apparently never performed.

Underneath Simon and Pi's name on the label was a little legend stating: "Arranged and produced by Mark P. Wirtz as a tribute to Phil Spector." Sure enough, Wirtz had tried all the tricks with the strings and rhythm section and produced a very acceptable pastiche which reawakened memories of the glory that had been Philles. Mark Wirtz has since disappeared, but some of us will always remember him for that fine gesture.

In summary, it can be said that Spector opened the door to what is happening today, and that if his style was never copied exactly as everybody else's had been, then that's mostly because it is impossible to recreate with any verisimilitude. In an age of plagiarists, that itself is a giant tribute.

8

HERB, JERRY ... AND PHIL
"Just an obligation ...."

FOR TWO YEARS PHIL SPECTOR WAS LOST FROM view. His name was seldom mentioned around the business, although there was a small ripple of interest, centered mainly around a few fanatics, when "I'll Never Need More Than This" made its appearance on a non-chart single in Britain, in 1967.

As late as the Spring of '69, I remember hearing someone in the business telling me a wild tale of Phil's life in the desert and his infrequent visits to Los Angeles. When he arrived in LA, my informant whispered, he would charge up Sunset Boulevard on a big Harley hog, wearing his funky old jeans and a sweatshirt, storm into his office, and demand a few thousand bucks. He would then vanish again, and nobody would see him for several more weeks, until he returned for a similar reason. Although probably nonsense, it was at least nice to hear Phil's name again, and reassuring to receive confirmation that somewhere on the planet those weird little gray cells were still pulsating. While there was life, one reasoned, there was always a chance he might explode upon us once again.

As it turned out, there was not long to wait. In March of '69, two records were released on the A & M label which signified the resurrection of the prophet. They were "You Came, You Saw, You Conquered" by the

Ronettes "featuring the Voice of Veronica," and "Love Is All I Have to Give" by a group called The Checkmates Ltd. The label on both records carried, in addition to the standard A & M logo, a symbol of a small man in a cloak and a top hat (guess who?) with the words "Phil Spector Productions" in typically elegant typeface and purple ink. He was back because, he said, "I got it in my bones again. I was getting very bored with what I heard on the radio, with everybody's nightmares and stuff."

He was not exactly greeted with open arms. His deal with Herb Alpert and Jerry Moss (the "A" and the "M" of A & M) ensured that some degree of ceremony would surround his new recordings, but all the advertising and all the prestige in the world couldn't shift Ronnie into the chart this time around—and the Checkmates Ltd. climbed no higher than number 65 in Billboard. The new era was off to a bad start.

It was particularly unfortunate because the records were definitely up to scratch, even though they weren't the revelations that two years of inactivity might have fomented. Spector had co-written Ronnie's record with a new team, Toni Wine and Irwin Levine from New York. Miss Wine had written, some years earlier, an excellent song for Patti LaBelle and the Bluebelles, called "Groovy

Kind Of Love." With "You Came, You Saw, You Conquered," Spector/Wine/Levine were off to a start which
seemed to promise a return to the halcyon days of the
partnerships with Gerry and Carole, Barry and Cynthia,
and Jeff and Ellie. The fact that Larry Levine was now
chief engineer at A & M's studios, where the record was
cut, appeared only to strengthen the auspicious feelings.

The record itself certainly sounded good. Starting
with a slightly out-of-character grunting bass guitar, it gives
its producer's identity away within seconds: already at the
third bar, when the jangling pianos enter, and again
at the end of the sixth, when the drummer goes to his
tom-toms and plays a rolling fill which could only have
come out of one head. The song is jaunty, strutting and
happy, and Ronnie does it justice, quivering away at the
"oh-ohhh" bits over the instrumental bridge. The strings
range almost out of the human aural spectrum, soaring
through Perry Botkin's admirable arrangement in company with a thicket of background voices—these voices
were definitely not the original Ronettes, but probably a
combination of LA session singers including the Checkmates and the Blossoms, with Darlene Love. One imagines
that Phil put the record out under the Ronettes' name
because of his previous failure with the Veronica debut
single—he may have also figured that DJ's would grab
onto a new Ronettes' cut as something to seize listeners'
interest. Something like: "Hey, remember 'Be my baby'
and 'Baby I love you'? Well, the gals who made those plat-
ters, the Ronettes, are back! And here's their first record
in many years, waxed by ace master super-producer Phil
Spector. . . ." That's probably the way Phil hoped it would
go. It didn't.

Perhaps its failure was a case of poetic justice, since
Phil was up to his old tricks again. On the B side Phil

had put no brand-spanking-new 1969 Spectorepic, but our old friend, the Jeff Barry produced "I Can Hear Music," the very *last* Ronettes record. What was he thinking of? Couldn't he get out of that 1963 mentality of putting crap on the backside? Even a rubbishy instrumental would have been better, as long as it was *new*. But to put out "I Can Hear Music" again . . . it just seemed too outrageous and cynically manipulative. And that was the end of Veronica on A & M.

The Checkmates Ltd., though, lasted quite a while longer. Made up of black singers Bobby Stevens and Sonny Charles, with Harvey Trees (guitar), Bill Van Buskirk (bass), and Sweet Louie (drums), they had been around for a long time. Fairly representative of their pre-Spector efforts is *The Checkmates Ltd. Live! At Caesar's Palace*, on Capitol. The sleeve bore tributes to the group from such well known Top 40 personalities as Shelley Berman, Nancy Wilson, Woody Allen, the Smothers Brothers, and Sammy Davis Jr.—aptly, as the album was recorded in Las Vegas.

Despite the diamonds-and-pearls atmosphere the record is great. Charles and Stevens keep the show going at a phenomenal pace, alternately knocking the audience out with a sledgehammer "Show Me" or a supersonic medley of R & B favorites like "Can I Get A Witness" and "Rockin' Robin," and setting them reeling with laughter with lightning-fast sketches on the racial situation—the Checkmates are a multiracial group. The atmosphere is tremendous: all those tuxedos and mink stoles are obviously having a ball. For music fans there's the bonus of Charles on the final brassy chorus of "Sunny," with a smashing imitation of the late Billy Stewart in his "Summertime" bag. They also do "You've Lost That Lovin' Feelin'," and despite the occasional comedy interludes, they sing the song as well as, if not better than, the Righteous Brothers.

Their duets on the chorus are magnificently synchronized, enough to make you jump up and shout. Unfortunately their studio work, judging from their two Capitol singles "Do The Walk" and "Mastered In the Art of Love," was very run-of-the-mill commercial R & B, overarranged and styled, not particularly well, for the discotheque.

Still, one has to remember that the Righteous Brothers' aesthetic beginnings were also humble, and it's more than likely that Spector had the Brothers in mind when he decided to use the Checkmates. The two sets of singers paralleled each other in many ways: Stevens was Medley, deep and dark and sonorous, while Charles was Hatfield, screaming at the upper end of the male vocal range, with a much lighter touch than his partner. It would be easy to say that, because they were black, Stevens and Charles were much better than Medley and Hatfield. But comparisons are pretty odious.

Stevens had a hand in writing some of the group's early material, and jointly authored "Love Is All I Have To Give," with Phil. The introduction to this song is riveting: what sounds like a million mandolins enter, strumming furiously, while a choir hums in a dirge-like manner in the background. Stevens groans a few time, the orchestral texture lightens, and he moves into a song which is actually quite ordinary on its own. But the mandolin effect and the menacing percussion constantly lift the track, once again with Botkin's clean string-plus-choir adding dramatic contrast. Charles puts in an appearance, to trade whoops with Stevens in a storming mid-section.

Their next try, just one month later, had more success than the first. Billed this time as Sonny Charles and The Checkmates Ltd., Sonny took the lead on a truly superb Spector/Wine/Levine song called "Black Pearl." The first thing which grabbed the ear was, initially, the sound, but for once the words also demanded attention:

Black Pearl, precious little girl,
Let me put you up where you belong.
Black Pearl, pretty little girl,
You've been in the background much too long.
You've been working so hard your whole life through,
Tending other people's houses,
Raising up their children too.
How 'bout something for me and you?

1969 Rondor Music. Reprinted by permission.

The way Charles sings it, the lyric comes over as young, proud, and beautiful. It is a brilliant performance, as full of vocal fireworks as "River Deep." It was typical of the way Spector could extract a master performance from an artist with almost no track record or prior reputation at all. Charles will be lucky if he ever surpasses the way he sang "Black Pearl" that night at A & M.

His vocal is a jewel placed in the finest of settings. Phil uses a slow Baion rhythm in the basses, and outdoes himself in the production of the backing voices. These

Spector with Bobby Stevens and Sonny Charles of the Checkmates Ltd.—and their "Black Pearl" single.

are all-pervasive yet remote as well—like the Heavenly Host come down to sit in on the gig. In addition, Spector and Perry Botkin add a novel textural contrast in the final shout-up with the introduction of an electric piano soloing in gospelly runs underneath the vocal fade—an effective, almost revivalist touch.

As befits such a beauty of a record, it did fairly well—particularly when one takes into account the industry's indifferent attitude toward its prime creator. It first appeared in the Hot 100 on May 10; it stayed there 13 weeks, hitting number 13 at its peak. Significantly—in view of its lyric content—it also nudged the Top Ten in the R & B chart.

On September 13 the Checkmates' album appeared, entitled "Love Is All We Have To Give." It was immediately named a Billboard Pick, with the review comment: "Should prove an instant chart winner." "Black Pearl" 's success made that something of a safe prophecy—nevertheless it was not a chart winner. It stayed in the Top 200 albums a mere four weeks.

The album was a distinctly schizophrenic affair: the first side included the two singles, one single-to-be ("Proud Mary"), and a reworking of two R & B standards, "I Keep Forgettin'" and "Spanish Harlem." The other side was taken up entirely by "The *Hair* Anthology Suite," in which Phil took the five most popular songs from that musical and fused them together into an organic whole. His comments on this may be somewhat enlightening. After asserting that everything he did on A & M was "just an obligation," he continued: "If I was serious about the *Hair* thing, I'd have composed original songs and done 'em, but I wasn't that serious at all. I just wanted to get the obligation finished and done with."

In view of the scale of the whole undertaking, one

might well doubt the seriousness of those remarks. It is likely this statement was merely a personal rationalization of what must have been a failure for him. A man like Spector cannot accept failure as simply as most mortals—there has to be some *reason* for it, some outside factor. That is no condemnation at all—how else would a creative genius be able to live with public rejection, if he could not lay the blame all about him in other directions? Such rationalization, false as it may be, is crucial to his survival.

The suite is, in fact, monstrous. It comes as no surprise to learn that "every note of the music was brilliantly, ingeniously, and magically arranged by Dee Barton"—in Spector's words on the sleeve. Dee Barton is best known for his work with Stan Kenton in the early Sixties. Beginning as a trombonist, he soon switched to drums and arranging—at one point he composed and arranged an entire album for the Kenton orchestra. His work on the *Hair* songs is that of a typical Kenton alumnus: showy, a little flashy, technically daring in a straight sort of way, but ultimately overblown and empty. As a demonstration of the resources of a professional arranger, it may be superb, but, in emotional content, it doesn't come within a million miles of those simple string lines on the original "Spanish Harlem."

Soon after the record was made, Spector elaborated on his reasons for using Barton: "I had a certain idea for the album. I had talked with several arrangers, but I couldn't communicate with them. I wanted to do something which was way, way ahead of its time in the charts. And I knew of Dee through his work with Stan Kenton, so I approached him. It was important that Dee be out there with the musicians. It made it a lot easier for me on the sessions . . . there was just too much to watch.

"It's a total sound thing. I think people today, especially the younger people, enjoy sound. They think it's all in a twisted guitar or a reverb. But they don't know. This is total sound. I felt it should almost be an opera written for them . . . a suite for them. Not the way the Who did it, but a real suite. The only reason I took the *Hair* tunes is because they're so commercial.

"I don't particularly are for the *Hair* songs at all, and I've never heard the cast album, and I never heard a song from the album. I've never heard the 5th Dimension record . . . every time it was on the air, I immediately turned the radio off. I didn't want to be influenced by it. And Dee is a jazz arranger. This thing we were doing was something altogether unique. I asked him: 'Did you ever hear the *Hair* songs?' He didn't know whether to say yes or no, and he finally said: 'I've got to be honest with you . . . no.' I said great." (5)

The obviously serious intent displayed here measures up curiously against his later comments, and against this subsequent remark about the great "Black Pearl:" "It was serious to the extent that I went in and wrote a song that I knew was a hit, and I did it as a hit record. But other than that. . . ."

Drawbacks aside, Spector's suite still beats the official cast album cold. Charles and Stevens sing their guts out, and thus counteracting the orchestral opulence they make it into a listenable experience. Charles particularly cooks on "Let the Sunshine In." Still, the very mawkishness of the Ragni/Rado lyrics makes it positively embarrassing in places. Hearing Sonny wail on a line like "I got my liver," and try to make it convincing, makes one wish Spector had written the original material. Better still he could have used the studio time to make another couple of singles.

The fact that Barton was also the arranger on three other songs on the album—"Spanish Harlem," "Proud

Mary," and "I Keep Forgettin'"—may account for their disappointing low quality as well, though one hesitates to lay the blame at his feet. Spector has always been the sole arbiter of his own product. "Spanish Harlem" adds nothing to Ben E. King's original; instead it merely fattens the texture and thus loses the poignant sense of distance; "Proud Mary" is a choogling mess with a corny use of the chorus—one track on which the "bigness" doesn't work one bit. And "I Keep Forgettin'," which Leiber and Stoller wrote for Chuck Jackson back in '61—that record (Wand 126), got only to 55 in the chart, but it was one of the great avant-garde epics of its day—as far out as Bacharach's early productions with Dionne Warwick. Spector's treatment loses the freshness and adds nothing in recompense. "Proud Mary" was lifted from the album for a single which reached no higher than 69 in November.

There is a curious sidelight to Spector's involvement with the Checkmates. Even in 1969, he had trouble getting "Black Pearl played: "When it came out, white guys wouldn't play it because their attitude was 'I'll be damned I'm gonna give credence to any nigger. Like I'll be damned if I'm gonna make any black pearls for these people.' And the black people said, 'Well, man, some honkey's made it. Why should we play it? Maybe it'll start trouble in the area—maybe somebody will bomb our station if we play it.' We got some very nasty letters on that record." (6) Here was Ike and Tina Turner all over again, and this sideways racism must have given the producer a large and uncomfortable sense of *déjà vu*.

Perhaps Larry Levine has made the most significant comment yet on the saga of Spector and A & M: that the Checkmates album was probably the fastest album Phil ever did. And Phil is not noted for being the speediest worker around when he's trying hard.

The same week that the Checkmates' album appeared, A & M and Spector also released the *River Deep–Mountain High* album for the first time in America. Unlike the first British pressing, the sleeve bore two legends: the first, printed over the title on the cover, read: "An Historic Recording by Phil Spector;" the second, a little sticker on the front, said: " 'River Deep—Mountain High' is a perfect record from start to finish. You couldn't improve on it." It was signed by George Harrison—even at this stage, just putting it out wasn't enough. The stigma still needed to be purged through the accolades of superstars.

There was one significant change from the original British issue: the Turner-produced "You're So Fine" had been dropped and replaced by "River Deep"'s sister song, "I'll Never Need More Than This." It was a handsome swap—the album went to 102 in the pop album chart, and 37 in the R & B list.

But Spector's involvement with the label was finished. Once again he seemed in limbo. Around this time Levine remarked: "I don't know what he's going to do now. He doesn't have a contract with A & M, but we're

trying to work something out whereby he can use our studios.

"He can do anything if he wants to do it bad enough, but I don't think he's hungry enough to try hard now. In the old days he used to drive himself really hard, trying to prove to himself that he was the best, but you never prove that to yourself and eventually he got hung up on the image that was built around him. But if he ever wants to, he can make it back again."

Levine was right, though he cannot have had any premonition of the events which were to lead Spector to "make it back again," into the most controversial period of an already stormy career.

9

LET IT BE
"'How Spector ruined
the Beatles'... ha!"

AT THE BEGINNING OF 1970, THE BEATLES WERE in disarray. It had become obvious that *Abbey Road* would be their last studio statement as a unit. Paul, completely out of it, was working on his first solo album; John had just released the magnificent "Cold Turkey," following "Give Peace A Chance," which set the whole world singing; Ringo had made the disastrous *Sentimental Journey* album, which could only have been intended as a present for his parents; and George, although "Something" had been a huge success, still seemed restricted to B sides and two cuts per album.

A few months earlier, the group as a whole had released one of their best singles, "Get Back." A rocking, bluesy McCartney song, it hammered home the message of its title: the record was an obvious reversion to pre-*Rubber Soul* days, when their work in the studio was roughly comparable to what they played on stage. The addition of Billy Preston on electric piano meant no overdubbing was required, and the track had an unmistakably "live" feel.

It was rumored that the song came from a movie called *Get Back With The Beatles*, from which an album would also appear. It was said the film had been made to display the group at work in the studio, in "real" conditions instead of the artificial lip-synching of their early screen appearances. This rumor preceded *Abbey Road*, and the appearance of the latter was something of a surprise. What had happened to the *Get Back* album, not to mention the movie?

Some time around the end of '69, the Beatles met Spector once again—the first real meeting since the concurrent heydeys of Beatlemania and the Philles label. Lennon remembers that the meeting came at the behest of the Beatles' busines manager, Allen Klein. "Allen, Yoko and I had been talking about him. He'd had some kind of relationship with Allen, not a business one . . . or maybe it was. Anyway, they knew each other, and Klein really put us together. That's one of Allen's arts, bringing people together. It's like a patron in the Arts. I mean, patrons used to get their percentages as well. . . . It's the same kind of thing."

The immediate result of the rendezvous was twofold: Spector was given the *Get Back* album to remix and generally put into shape for release, and he was called in on a session for a new single by Lennon and the Plastic Ono Band.

Most people in Lennon's position would have carried on producing themselves, that being part of the current fashion of self-expression which had engulfed rock. Why did he want Spector in?

"Well I produced 'Give Peace A Chance' in a bedroom, so that's all right. Then when we did 'Cold Turkey,' it took longer than it should take because I'd have to be in the room playing it, and then I'd have to run into the next room. . . . I still go in and check the bass and the bass drum and all that, but I can at least relax when I'm trying to play my instrument. When you produce it yourself, you've really got to be doing two things at once. Yoko could help me with voice and instruments, but some of the technical things she just doesn't know about, especially in those days. It's nice to work with somebody. He's just great, and my ego's not that big that I can't stand to have somebody else on a record with me, if they're doing what I like. I could tell by the sound he made on those great records . . . that's the kind of sound I like. It's not necessarily that I want the Ronettes or 'Da Doo Ron Ron' on every track, but I knew that here was somebody I could work with who could make that particular sound, especially that big one that didn't make it in America but was great . . . Ike and Tina Turner. Anybody who could make that *must* be fantastic.

"Of course, (as the Beatles) we'd thought that if we ever used anybody besides George Martin, it would be Phil. Obviously we'd discussed not using George, even when we'd used him, just for a change. America being the dream place, we were always suspicious that American studios were much better than ours, than EMI. It wasn't so true, of course, when we got over there. It was just that the early Sun records were something special, and a few records that Spector and some other people had made. It was usually the man, and not the studio. So we often talked about Spector, that we'd like to work with him, but it was on and off for years."

The chemistry was just right between Phil and John.

They shared the same primary influence: those "yellow Sun records from Memphis" that John Sebastian sang about in "Nashville Cats." At heart they were both old rockers, in love with tape echo and a cracking backbeat on the drum. They had similar roots, they had both passed through everything at one time or another, and they could communicate. Spector was never given to working with established artists, but the Beatles were just right for him. Outside of Elvis and Dylan (both of whom he has expressed a wish to produce), the Beatles were probably the only big name he would have consented to work with. Spector himself places the strength of their relationship in that "neither of us is making the other one. No one's on a free ride. There's mutual respect and all that. I love them, I think they're really great. They really know what's going on, they understand. I like it because when they work, they work very hard, and they're very, very talented. They set quite a mark, y'know, they really did."

Even more revealing, he added: "Then, of course, by working with them I don't have to get wrapped up in the fact that I did 'Lovin' Feelin' ' and 'River Deep' and how'm I ever going to achieve something more spectacular than that? With them as a vehicle I can achieve it but not have to worry about proving it again." For the first time in years perhaps, Spector saw a chink of light which indicated an unfamiliar state: peace of mind. It looked as though he could relax at last, while still giving his best.

His first concrete collaboration with Lennon was "Instant Karma," released on February 9, 1970. The session had taken place only a few weeks earlier at EMI's Abbey Road studio. The musicians were the original Plastic Ono Band, the one which played the Toronto Festival gig recorded as *Live Peace In Toronto 1969*, except that George

Harrison had replaced Eric Clapton. Klaus Voorman, an old friend from Hamburg who had drawn the *Revolver* cover and been a member of the Brian Epstein-managed group Paddy, Klaus, and Gibson, played bass; Alan White, a former member of the Alan Price Set, was on drums; while John and George messed around with pianos and guitars.

It was a surprise session, typical of those days. Alan White remembers getting a phone call that day, saying that John wanted to do a session at EMI, and White "just turned up." According to John, Spector was absent as the evening began. "We were playing, and we weren't getting very far," he remembers. "I knew I had a hit record. I'd

JOHN ONO LENNON
INSTANT KARMA!
(WE ALL SHINE ON)

PRODUCED BY
PHIL SPECTOR
APPLE RECORDS 1818

written it that morning, and I knew I had it, but it would've taken me a couple of days to make, building up and building up and running between the two rooms. That way, it might have turned out very heavy and funky, like 'Cold Turkey,' but then Spector walked in." They carried on with the song, running it down and trying takes. "Suddenly when we went in the room and heard what he'd done to it . . . it was fantastic. It sounded like there was fifty people playing."

What Spector had done was to mold, ever so subtly, what the musicians were doing. He had put John on one grand piano, White and Harrison playing opposite ends of the keyboard of another, and Voorman on electric piano. For the drums, he had placed a towel over the floor tom-tom and made White play his fills at breakneck tempo, punctuating the song like a pneumatic road drill on a quiet Sunday afternoon. After they had laid down the track and vocal, they decided they needed a choir. A few of them piled into a car, drove into central London to a discotheque, and dragged people out to the studio to sing the infectious chorus, "All shine on . . . like the moon and the stars and the sun," behind John.

But it was the sound which sold the record. No Beatles record had ever possessed such a unique sound; Spector had used echo to make the drums reverberate like someone slapping a wet fish on a marble slab, and the voices sounded hollow and decayed. He'd accentuated the characteristics of Lennon's voice, making it older and more cracked than ever before. It was, above all, such a *simple* record. All that sophistication had produced a sound as primitive and joyous as an old-time jug band. It must have been just the sound that John, without knowing it, had been looking for.

But Spector didn't want to stop. "He wanted to

go on with it," John says, "putting more people on it. Now the only thing I ever do with Spector is stop him, because otherwise he'd go on and on and there'd be nothing left. That time, I didn't let him. I knew that was it. But he was saying, 'Are you sure? I'd just like to put violins on, on the West Coast.' But I said no, and we put it out."

Still, if you lived in Britain at that time, the "Instant Karma" you heard was not the one which crashed the American charts. It was slightly rougher than the U.S. recording, harsher and more direct. In fact it was the original mix, okayed by John. So what was the American record?

"Spector sneakily remixed it in the States," John says with a wry grin. "He put a cleaner version out, without telling me. It's the only time anyone's done *that*." The fact that the Lennon/Spector relationship continued unharmed is surely eloquent tribute to John's respect for Phil. If anyone else had remixed Lennon's record, one shudders to imagine the consequences. What's more, Phil had also scratched a message in the run-off groove: "PHIL & RONNIE," it said.

For Spector, the entire "Karma" session had been a rejuvenation. "It was just four people," he says, "and it brought back the days of 'To Know Him Is To Love Him.' You see, I was never a stereo bug. I don't like stereo, maybe because none of my old records were. I can't make stereo out of them now, because all that whole track, that massive track, was cut on one track, and I can't stereo it. I think in terms of a single record being monaural. Stereo seems to take something away from it."

"Karma" was well received by the public and industry, but made no more waves than the average ex-Beatle smash hit. Three weeks later, there was a new official Beatles single: "Let It Be." Rumor now had it that this was the official title of the next movie/album, both resurrected for imminent release.

The single of "Let It Be" was an obvious McCartney song, a piece of White Gospel with chunky piano, background choir, and very little rhythm section. Mid-way appeared a guitar solo which sounded as if it had been put through a Leslie speaker; highly distorted, it was still more functional than distinguished. The record was a typical George Martin production. Martin was fine when the Beatles wanted to develop new techniques for particular songs, like the circus noises on "Mr. Kite" and the tape loops on "Tomorrow Never Knows." His background in novelty and comedy records gave him a wide knowledge of studio effects, and he was an imaginative arranger—consequently he was ideal while the group remained in their learning stage, groping for new possibilities and badly needing someone to guide them.

But when it came to getting a fat, funky rock and roll sound, the essential ingredient in the bulk of their work, Martin was no better than any other record company staff producer. He wasn't bad, but he tended to leave the sound "dry" and ordinary. Honest as it was in its rather old-fashioned way, this technique was not enough for an era when anyone could hear the tough sound that Levon Helm, The Band's drummer, was getting on their albums.

Martin and Glyn Johns had recorded all the material from the *Get Back* film sessions in the first two weeks of January, 1969. As befitted the original conception, the tapes were all a bit rough, like rehearsals or demo tapes, or just good old jam sessions. At that stage they were not really intended as anything more.

When, in May, the *Let It Be* album came out, George Martin must have had a hell of a shock. The album bore practically no resemblance at all to the music he had taped 16 months before. The reason was one man: Phil Spector. Martin did not like what he heard, and neither did the media, whose critics lined up to sling mud at it. The *Rolling*

Stone review, reproduced here in its entirety, is just one example of how people grabbed at the chance to let fly their deepest invective. The target was always Spector, "the interloper." Phil is understandably more than a little bitter about the incident.

"Critically, I was destroyed . . . they just panned the shit out of me. It was fun to see people getting into it . . . 'how Spector ruined the Beatles' and how I took all the guts out of them. Now that it's sold three million, and it's all over and done with, they should listen to what was there beforehand, I mean *really* listen to it. The Beatles didn't want it out. That was never brought up in the reviews. If the Beatles had wanted it out, they would never have asked me to do it. But they were ashamed of the album, they hated the album, and there was a lot of work in editing and putting things together. We spent weeks on that album, really, just putting it together and overdubbing strings. And then, in the end, they said, 'You can be the final judge of it, if you like, because we're really not involved in it and we don't like it any more.' I said no, you be the final judges, and every one of them sent me a telegram saying, 'It's great, this is okay, you're taking a great burden off us all.'

"I just figured that it's the public, your fans y'know, they can't wait to have you back, and then as soon as you come back they just destroy the shit out of you. I think everybody resented that it was the Beatles. And there was also the fact that most of the reviews were written by English people, picked up by the American Press, and the English were a bit resentful of an American, I don't care who it was, an American coming in, taking over.

"They don't know that it was no favor to me to give me George Martin's job, because I don't consider myself in the same situation or league. . . . I don't consider

RECORDS

LET IT BE, The Beatles *(Apple AR 3400)*

To those who found their work since the white album as emotionally vapid as it was technically breathtaking, the news that the Beatles were about to bestow on us an album full of gems they'd never gotten around to polishing beyond recognition was most encouraging. Who among us, after all, wouldn't have preferred a good old slipshod "Save The Last Dance For Me" to the self-conscious and lifeless "Oh! Darlin'" they'd been dealing in?

Well, it was too good to be true—somebody apparently just couldn't Let It Be, with the result that they put the load on their new friend P. Spector, who in turn whipped out his orchestra and choir and proceeded to turn several of the rough gems on the best Beatle album in ages into costume jewelry.

Granted that he would have preferred to have been in on the project from its inception rather than having it all handed to him eight months after its announced release date (in which case we would never have been led to expect spontaneity and his reputation would still be intact), one can't help but wonder why he involved himself at all, and wonder also, how he came to the conclusion that lavish decoration of several of the tracks would enhance the straightforwardness of the album.

To Phil Spector, stinging slaps on both wrists.

He's rendered "The Long and Winding Road," for instance, virtually unlistenable with hideously cloying strings and a ridiculous choir that serve only to accentuate the listlessness of Paul's vocal and the song's potential for further mutilation at the hands of the countless schlock-mongers who will undoubtedly trip all over one another in their haste to cover it. A slightly lesser chapter in the ongoing story of McCartney as facile romanticist, it might have eventually begun to grow on one as unassumingly charming, had not Spector felt compelled to transform an apparently early take into an extravaganza of oppressive mush. Sure, he was just trying to help it along, but Spectorized it evokes nothing so much as dewey-eyed little Mark Lester warbling his waif's heart out amidst the assembled *Oliver* orchestra and choir.

"I Me Mine," the waltz sections of which reminds one very definitely of something from one of *The Al Jolson Story's* more maudlin moments, almost benefits from such treatment—it would have been fully as hilarious as "Good Night," after all, had Spector obscured its raunchy guitar with the gooey strings he's so generously lavished on the rest of it. As he's left it, though, it, like "Winding Road," is funny enough to find cloying but not funny enough to enjoy laughing at.

Elsewhere, Spector compounds his mush fixation with an inability to choose the right take (it is said that nothing on the "official album" comes from the actual film sessions, mind you). Inexplicably dissatisfied with the single version of "Let It Be," for instance, he hunted up a take in which some jagged guitar and absurdly inappropriate percussion almost capsize the whole affair, decided that it might be real Class to orchestrally embellish the vocal, and thus dubbed in—yes!—brass. Here the effect isn't even humorous—Spector was apparently too intent on remembering how the horns went on "Hey Jude" to listen closely enough to this one to realize that they're about as appropriate here as piccoloes would have been on "Helter Skeltre."

Happily though, he didn't impose himself too offensively on anything else, and much of what remains is splendid indeed:

Like John's "All Across The Universe," which, like "Julia," is dreamy, childlike, and dramatic all at once and contains both an unusually inventive melody and tender devotional vocal.

Like the two rough-honed rockers, the crudely revival-ish "I've Got A Feeling" and "One After 909," both of which are as much fun to listen to as they apparently were to make. "C'mon, baby, don't be cold as ice" may be at once the most ridiculous and magnificent line Lennon-McCartney ever wrote.

Like John's crossword-puzzlish "Dig a Pony," which features an urgent old rocker's vocal and, being very much in the same vein as such earlier Lennonisms as "Happiness Is a Warm Gun," nearly makes up for the absence of "Don't Let Me Down" and "The Last Dance."

And especially like everyone's two favorites, "Two of Us," which is at once infectiously rhythmic and irresistibly lilting in the grand tradition of "I'll Follow the Sun," and the magnificent chunky, thumping, and subtly skiffy "Get Back," which here lacks an ending but still contains delightful comping by John and Billy Preston.

All of these are, of course, available on the bootleg versions of the album, a further advantage of which is their pure unSpectoredness and the presence of various goodies that didn't quite make it to the official release.

Musically, boys, you passed the audition. In terms of having the judgment to avoid either over-producing yourselves or casting the fate of your get-back statement to the most notorious of all over-producers, you didn't. Which somehow doesn't seem to matter much any more anyway.   JOHN MENDELSOHN

Well, by now you've probably heard the official album, admired the production, and scowled at its lack of balls. The bootlegs are of varying quality, have different takes, and cost about the same. The one here is the best we've heard, as well as one of the most complete, and it'll do until George Martin gets around to putting out a bootleg of what it *should* have sounded like.   ED WARD

Rolling Stone's review of the "Let It Be" album—perhaps the foremost example of the way Spector was criticised for his "re-production" work on the record.

him with me. He's somewhere else. He's an arranger, that's all. As far as *Let It Be*, he had left it in a deplorable condition, and it was not satisfactory to any of them, they did not want it out as it was. So John said, 'Let Phil do it,' and I said, 'Fine.' Then I said, 'Would anybody like to get involved in it, work on it with me?' 'No.' George came down a couple of times to listen, Ringo came down and overdubbed drum, John said, 'Send me an acetate when it's finished,' Paul the same thing, and that was it. They didn't care. But they did have the right to say 'We don't want it out,' and they didn't say that. In five years from now, maybe people will understand how good the material was.

"But at that time everyone was saying, 'Oh Beatles, don't break up, give us something else to remember you by,' and you give it to them and then the critics just knock the shit out of it. 'It's awful, it's this, it's that . . . but it's your Beatles, *your great Beatles!* Forget my name . . . if my name hadn't been on the album, there wouldn't have been all that. George told me that, John, everyone . . . that's the dues you have to pay. It was nothing to me . . . I had my reputation before the Beatles were around. I'm not over-cocky or anything, but they know that and I certainly knew that. I knew who I was and what I was before I met the Beatles."

Most of the critical controversy centered around a McCartney song called "The Long And Winding Road," a typical Paul ballad with a long and winding tune. By the time the album came out, original versions of the songs had already been pressed and sold on bootleg albums—so most of the people who wrote about *Let It Be* had heard the pre-Spector mixes, and knew that Phil had added strings, voices, harp, and drums to "The Long And Winding Road." They hated it, calling it trash, schmaltz worthy of Lawrence Welk, and all kind of things. Whereas George Martin had counteracted Paul's romantic tendencies by creating very dry surroundings for his songs (like the vibratoless string quartet on "Yesterday"), Spector was taking McCartney at his face value, and highlighting what was already there. It is possible that this track, above all others, epitomizes Paul McCartney. That is not meant to be derogatory: to hear those strings sweeping in after the first line of vocal is to hear a kind of beauty which the original Martin-produced track just doesn't have.

Paul, at that time trying to extricate himself from the whole Apple/Klein/Beatles situation, did not enjoy the new version one bit. In fact, when he took the Beatles to court a few months later, he used the track as an example of how they were trying to ruin his reputation. Paul hated the whole album, particularly the blurb at the top of the back cover: "This is a new phase Beatles album. . . . Essential to the content of the film *Let It Be* was that they performed live for many of the tracks; in comes the warmth and the freshness of a live performance; as reproduced for disk by Phil Spector." He pointed out that no other Beatles record had ever needed such a blatant piece of hype. The problem here was one of misunderstanding; Spector cared little about pretensions to a "live" feeling—he just tried to make it as good as he possibly could. And to him that meant, at least some of the time, embellishment and bigness.

"[Paul] took the Grammy for it, though," Spector replies sarcastically to McCartney's criticism. "He went and picked the Grammy up, for the album that he didn't want out, supposedly that we used to ruin him artistically . . . what did he pick the Grammy up for? Silly. And in many respects it ended the Beatle Era really good, because 'The Long and Winding Road' is a good way for the Beatles

to go out, you know what I mean? It all made sense . . .
'The Long and Winding Road' . . . it was sort of what
they'd lived through. It was a typical Paul song, that's the
way I heard it and that's the way I did it, and they gave
me freedom to do what I wanted. As far as I'm concerned,
George and John and Ringo have just as much say as Paul
does, and Paul was asked a hundred times if he wanted
to become more involved in it, and he said 'No.' I think
he just used it as an argument. I guess if I were his attorneys,
I'd tell him the same thing: 'Look what they've done, they've
taken it out of your songs.' It didn't matter that he refused
to work on it, and that the album never would have come
out. A lot of people could say, 'So what if it never came
out?' but in the end the Beatles said okay, they wanted
the album out that way. They listened, and they could
have said, 'No, we don't want out name on it.' It's their
name. And I didn't need all of what happened after
that. . . . I mean, Time Magazine called it The Spectre
of The Beatles. It was a field day."

On the "Let It Be" song, Spector had done a complete re-production job. He had beefed up the whole take,
creating a bigger voice sound to emphasize the churchy
aspect of the tune. He also added some fantastic out-take
guitar from George, both behind Paul and in a short,
scorching solo. But what attracted most criticism on the
track was the percussion. Spector put tape echo on the
hi-hat cymbals, to add a gentle "shushing" sound behind
the exposed vocal. In fact the hi-hat is probably a little
too prominent throughout the track. If he had mixed it
down just a little more then no one would have noticed.
There is also some brass added, but it is at worst inoffensive
and at best well in keeping with the general tone. Lennon
admits he thought Phil got "a bit fruity" on this one, though.

Spector saved his best job for "Across The Universe,"

a Lennon song from their Indian period which had been hanging around in rough form for some time and which made its first appearance as the Beatles' contribution to a charity record for the World Wildlife Fund (ironically, this same organization inspired the title, *Wild Life*, of the first album from Paul's band, Wings, late in 1971).

John thinks Spector "worked wonders on ['Across The Universe']. The original track was a real sorry bit of shit. I was singing out of tune, and instead of getting a decent choir, we got fans from outside . . . Apple Scruffs or whatever you call them. They came in and they were singing all off-key. Nobody was interested in doing the tune, originally, . . . they were all sick. It's sort of subliminal, . . . the tune was really good, and I think that, subliminally, people don't want to work with you sometimes. It got screwed up. That happens. . . . I've been the cause of a situation like that, too, so it isn't all one-sided. Phil slowed the whole tape down, added the strings . . . he did a really special job.

"I only ever listened to the *Let It Be* album once, I never got into it, but I thought that it was great. I thought that all those ordinary tracks, the rocky ones, were all saved well. Just a bit fruity on 'Let It Be,' but nothing to scream about . . . he was just having some fun, I think, because he'd had such a shitty job, with no help really. And 'The Long and Winding Road' I think was . . . good."

"Get Back" was also included on the album. Phil had chosen the take from the famous concert on the roof of Apple's London headquarters, January 30, 1969. Just as good as the single, with Billy Preston still on electric piano, it is here presented complete with John's final shout to the small audience: "I'd like to say Thank You on behalf of the group, and I hope we passed the audition."

After "Universe," perhaps the best treatment was

given George's unusual song, "I Me Mine." Spector puts strings on here, too, and imbues the track with a luster which foreshadows their later work together. Nevertheless, it was with a heavy symbolism that designer John Kosh put the record in a black sleeve, with separate photographs of the four musicians.

Finally, two verdicts on the album: "I was so relieved, because I'd got so miserable about the whole damn thing"—Lennon; and "It was like being back again"—Spector.

For seven years, George Harrison was just about the most frustrated composer in the whole world. Every time a new Beatles album came out, there were two Harrison songs on it; though by the time of the "White Album," it was obvious he had much more to say than the space allotted him. He just did not have an outlet for it. At that time, it was not really imaginable for a Beatle to release a solo album of his own *songs.* Any extramural project was, by unspoken convention, something else—like John's *Life with the Lions* and *Two Virgins* albums. George went this route too, with *Electronic Sound*, recorded after he had learned how to make his Moog synthesizer hiss and squeal.

Harrison spent most of 1970 in the studio, working at a three-record album which would finally provide him the required outlet. *All Things Must Pass* came out November 27, 1970. Harrison had worked, of course, with Spector—Lennon, when he heard of it, had fears for the partnership: "George likes to go on and on arranging things, and Phil likes to go on and on adding things, so they've got to watch that when they get together, because they'll just end up in . . . I don't know." Harrison's notorious tendency to perfectionism, combined with Phil's love of overdubbing, explains why the album was so long in the making once it had been started. Why a three-record set? Lennon again: "George just wanted to allow himself to expand and breathe, after being suppressed for so long."

The record was acclaimed as if it were a brand new Beatle album from their greatest days. It displayed, in fact, more Beatle-like characteristics than any of the solo albums from John or Paul, whose writing had been originally responsible for the group's sound. Somehow Harrison managed to combine the melodic flair of each: Paul's lyricism etched with the touch of John's acid, and an unmistakably Beatlesque voice and guitar. More than either Lennon or McCartney, Harrison concentrated on pure joyful

"George Harrison, listens to master tape of his first solo album, 'All Things Must Pass,' in recording studio with Pete Bennett (L) of Apple Records and Producer Phil Spector." (Courtesy of UPI).

melodies—the kind of songs that had made the group so loved.

The songs were by and large so strong that even without Spector, it would have been a fine record. But the producer stamps his personality all over it—and fortunately it gells just fine. George had often shown signs of needing someone to give his songs a setting. Some, like "If I Needed Someone" and "While My Guitar Gently Weeps," were just fine as small-group performances, but "Old Brown Shoe" and a few others needed a certain *oomph.* And that's what Spector gives him here.

Take, for instance, "Awaiting On You All." Looked at dispassionately, it's simply a remake of "River Deep—Mountain High" (Remember George's little benediction on the Ike and Tina album cover?), though the feeling is essentially different. Just listen to the leaping guitar/bass riff which opens the cut, or the great contrasting rhythms on maracas and tambourine, or the guitars sliding down at the end of each chorus over the maracas, before being cut off sharp by one of those cosmic thumps; and imagine this song as if it had been written for and played on, say, the *Abbey Road* album as a straight funky rocker. Then you'll realize the difference Phil Spector can make to a record.

Spector's trademarks fill the grooves to almost overflowing. On the rhythm track of "Isn't It A Pity" you can hear unnumbered acoustic rhythm guitars, all strumming lightly on the beat, giving the cut its body and lift. Those guitars were played by the members of Badfinger, the Apple group formerly known as the Ivies, providing that lower stratum of rhythm and harmony which is felt rather than perceived.

"Let It Down," the record's most utterly thrilling track, picks you up in the best Spector tradition and never lets you down until you hear the hiss of the separation band. The tension built between the subdued, reverential verses and the roaring chorus is electrifying, as is the tape echo on the hi-hat. Arranger John Barham and Spector manage to extract a very unusual texture from the combined strings and horns of Bobby Keys (tenor) and Jim Price (trumpet), and add an organ (either Billy Preston or Gary Wright) to top it off. "What Is Life?", another mover, starts off in a great groove reminiscent of the Ronettes and "Baby I Love You," with romping horns and all.

However, lest anyone get the impression that this is simply a Spector record with George Harrison on vocals and guitar, Spector consistently proves here just how sympathetic to the performer he can be. The sound he gets for George on the acoustic "Apple Scruffs" is bright, crisp, and shining, while Country songs like "If Not For You" and "Behind That Locked Door" are given a mellow, autumnal mix. The steel guitar of Nashville veteran Pete Drake was surely never more advantageously displayed than on the latter cut.

The best track of all, "Beware of Darkness," has all of George's talents on display and almost none of his failings. Here he employs a knack usually reserved by McCartney—starting a song on a note one doesn't expect. The whole tune is gorgeous, enhanced by some of the finest guitar licks ever played. Apart from a crystal clear sound, the only evidence here of Spector is a delicate whisper of strings.

An unusual facet of the album is the almost complete homogeneity of the background voices, billed as the George O'Hara-Smith Singers. In fact they are all George overdubbed a few dozen times. The effect is dazzling, like the clearest of mirrors. There is, however, one other singer on the album. And thereby hangs an anecdote.

Tony Orlando was escorting his wife Elaine to a

record industry convention in America very early in 1971, when he bumped into Phil. Tony, who is now lead voice of the Top 40 group Dawn, then had a number one hit with "Knock Three Times"— and the single version of "My Sweet Lord" from *All Things Must Pass* was at number two. Phil, as is his wont, was bubbling over with success, and would talk of nothing but the Harrison record.

Eventually he looked closely at Tony and Elaine and said very seriously: "Yes, but didn't you listen to the background voices on 'My Sweet Lord'?" "Sure, Phil." "D'you know who it is?" "No, Phil." "That's ME in there, me singing behind George." To which Elaine, once Phil's secretary, replied: "Phil . . . once a Teddy Bear, always a Teddy Bear."

All Things Must Pass may well be the most perfectly mixed album of all time, but it can still be hard to take all at once. Listened to long and hard, the textures become too rich—as much the effect of George's predilection for preachy lyrics as of the production. However, it was an undeniable aesthetic and popular success, and it certainly served to bring George to a prominence which was, for him, unprecedented. It seemed almost the rock equivalent of the shock felt by pre-war moviegoers when Garbo first opened her mouth in a talkie: Garbo talks!—Harrison is free! As Phil said soon afterwards: "They appreciate that the album did a lot for George."

Well before *All Things Must Pass* was finished, in May of 1970, *Rolling Stone* reported that John Lennon had been staying with Phil Spector in the latter's home at the western end of Sunset Strip. A posse of Pinkerton guards patrolled the grounds, the magazine said, stopping even Bel Air policemen who got too close to the property—Phil's paranoia again. (After all, you can walk into

Apple's London office, even when all four Beatles are there, without even knocking.) *Rolling Stone* went on to report speculation that John and Yoko were there to receive treatment from the famous Californian analyst, Arthur Janov—as in fact they were.

The treatment had a profound effect on John. For years he had expressed his malice and inner rage through the overt imagery of songs like "I Am The Walrus" and "Julia," where meaning and intentions were buried beneath layers of dead skin. You had to dig to find out that "Julia" concerned his mother, and that "Walrus," although magnificent and a real Beatles classic, was essentially meaningless—the gesture of a man battering his head against a door, trying to break it down because he cannot find the handle.

John had been trying to find that handle all his performing life. His search expressed itself it many forms: most notably in violence inflicted on others both cerebrally and physically, in drugs, and his dalliance with the Maharishi, who turned out to be nothing more than Sexy Sadie.

Through Janov's concept of the Primal Scream, Lennon felt he had found the handle at last—the answer was total honesty. No longer could his music be "art;" his words must carry nothing but the most naked truth, the starkest expression of honesty. No more images, conscious or instinctive, could be allowed to get in the way of the message.

Janov's instructions gave birth to an album called *John Lennon/Plastic Ono Band*, released on December 7, 1970. The critics were awed—it was perhaps the greatest thing he had done. Still it was never terribly popular because it was just too naked, too hard to take for anyone who still clung to the notion that the ex-Beatles should *all* be making pretty music. Why couldn't John be like George, and write nice tunes like he used to?

Instead the songs were full of lines like: "I seen through junkies. I been through it all; I seen religion from Jesus to Paul" and "Keep you doped with religion and sex and TV, and you think you're so clever and classless and free." An attempt at total realism, it culminated in the faded, frightening vignette of "My Mummy's Dead," when John bared his pain for all to see. This was "Julia" without the concentration on making a pop record—the air of desperate introspection was genuinely scary.

Spector had a good deal to do with the ultimate sound of the record, though he was late arriving for the sessions and John became so impatient that he started cutting tracks without him. The overall sound is one of simplicity, concentrating on the flatness of the electric guitar, or the resonance of the grand piano. Lennon tells of the concept's formation: "I'd always played piano at home, and made tapes, and played guitar and made demos with double tracking, and when you're alone playing the piano with the loud pedal on, it really has a beautiful ringing thing . . . it's an orchestra in itself. So is a double-tracked guitar or a double-tracked voice. I'm also a great admirer of Lee Dorsey-type records, very simple, or even some James Brown, where there's very little going on, just a good beat, and so I wanted to do it like that.

"The words were so strong on most of it that orchestration would just have been added cream that you didn't need. It was really just tight production, a beautiful production, and the piano *does* ring . . . for anybody with ears, you can hear all the orchestration you want just in the echo on the pianos and the things that were there. I don't understand what people were shocked by . . . maybe it was me singing about my mother. It was like the Sun records; some of the Beatle records got spoiled by going past that. A lot of my tracks like 'Rain' and 'Ticket To Ride,' I tried to keep them simpl e. The White Album was simple. 'Mr. Kite' . . . there was very little on that, except for the freaky George Martin mad tape organ thing. Just bass drum, bass, and guitar. 'Sexy Sadie' and 'Yer Blues' were very simple tracks, just four people. That's what I wanted on this album."

He got it. On "Well Well Well" for instance, there are only three musicians—John (guitar), Klaus (bass guitar) and Ringo—but the textures and detail are breathtaking. The most evil guitar ever plays unison riffs with the voice while bass and bass drum thud together on the beat. Listening hard, you can even hear what sounds like the echo on Ringo's pedal return spring—rather like a death rattle. And the hi-hat on the chorus has so much solid echo that it's positively throaty.

The piano tracks are just as striking. John plays keyboard on "Remember"—the very rudimentary backing is as effective as anything could be in this context. Spector plays piano on "Love," mixing with John's soft-strumming acoustic guitar and voice. This record brings out the inherent tonal qualities of the piano whether in the poignant single chords of "Mother," crashing and fading and dying so slowly, or the cavernous, bible-black tone supplied by Spector on "Love."

All in all, it is a far out record from every angle—but no surprise that the Top 40 fans of America and Britain didn't take too kindly to it. The French, however, did. Ever on the side of the avant-gardist, they voted it best album of the year in one hip magazine poll.

🕃

During the early part of 1970, *All Things Must Pass*, and the single taken from it, "My Sweet Lord," were smash hits all over the world. This as much as anything else cemented the Apple/Spector relationship. He became virtual A & R head of the label, with no official title but the power of veto over all the label's products, with the exception of Paul McCartney. In 1971 he put the block on a new Badfinger single because he knew it wasn't strong enough to follow the group's hit record, "No Matter What."

In the months that followed the success of Harrison's record, he produced three singles for Apple: "Power To The People" by Lennon and the Plastic Ono Band, "Try Some, Buy Some" by his wife Ronnie, and "Bangla Desh" by Harrison.

"Power to the People" came soon after a Lennon interview in Red Mole, a British revolutionary newspaper. His interviewers, Tariq Ali and Robin Blackburn, former student leaders famous for their exploits in the days of '68, made the conversation almost totally political in content. "I just felt inspired by what they ⌊Ali and Blackburn⌋ said, although a lot of it's gobbledygook," John said in his dry, pragmatic way. "So I wrote 'Power to the People,' the same way as I wrote 'Give Peace A Chance,' as something for the people to sing. I make singles like broadsheets. It was another quickie, done at Ascot. It sounds like U.S. Bonds, with Fats Domino thrown in . . . straight rock. A bit scrappy, but it's not bad. I just wanted to say it. As Yoko says, 'The message is the medium.' Especially with singles. I have a different attitude to singles, they're really like messages. 'All You Need Is Love,' 'Happy Christmas,' they're just chants that anyone can sing along with."

"Power To The People" conformed to all specifications for a revolutionary singalong record. It opened with the sound of marching feet ("Spector's idea—that's what made it"—Lennon), and another choir dragged out of a discotheque in the middle of the night—"Karma" style. The title/slogan, set to two bars of melody, is repeated no less than 35 times in the record's 3 minutes and 15 seconds, and is so simple that no one could ever forget it. The verses did not really matter too much since the chorus was so memorable, but it's amusing to note that Lennon begins the first verse with the opening line from his old song "Revolution": "You say you want a revolution. . . ." On the White Album he followed that up with, "When you talk about destruction, don't you know that you can count me out"; now he screams: "You'd better get it on right away."

The musical difference betwen the old and new "Revolution" songs also speaks change: the White Album song had gently looping bass lines from Paul and lots of "ba-umm shooby-do-wah" in the background, but "Power To The People" is pure, raucous rock and roll, which might have been cut sometime between "Quarter to Three" and "School Is Out." The drums are again to the fore, and Bobby Keys' tenor sax supplies most of the instrumental interest. Keys is no King Curtis or Sam "The Man" Taylor, but he's been around a long time and he knows how to honk. His fills and solo here are reminiscent of Johnny and the Hurricanes, and they fit perfectly.

But all this was nothing against "Try Some, Buy Some." This record was obviously closer to Spector's heart than anything since . . . well, since the last Ronettes record. As Paul Case says: "Phil wants a hit record with Ronnie again more than anything in the world. I think he'd give up all his worldly possessions for that."

The record came about partly when George Harrison, who had liked Ronnie's voice ever since the old days, asked if he could write a song for her. He came up with

"Try Some," a pleasant but essentially ordinary tune which Phil took apart, rearranged, and stuck back together again as an orchestral masterpiece. And that's what makes this record so different: the essence is in the sound of the voice against the orchestra. The words, which appear a typically Georgian paean to his Lord, mean nothing in the context of the record as a whole. If the record can be said to have a failing, it is that Ronnie is given nothing to chew on emotionally. There's no sentiment for her to express, no teenage love or thrill of "walking in the rain"—she is simply required to be an instrument, a lead sonority, another tone color. And that, probably, is why it wasn't a hit.

It was wholly magnificent nonetheless. Ronnie says Phil used about 40 strings and "I don't know how many mandolins"—he makes them sweep and soar in great blocks of sound, pirouetting around each other in ultraslow motion. The orchestral section near the end is absolutely breathtaking: the arrangement has a geometrical logic which makes use of suspended rhythms drawn out to screaming point. The mandolins, strumming a unison line like Greek balalaikas, were a trademark of the record. Although pretty much everyone was awed by it, nobody played it. Ronnie, with a flash of real insight, had the last word: "It was kind of a weird song. I'm not in it very much . . . it's like a movie where the star only appears now and then. I don't know how much I like me not singing so much."

Phil's eternal trust in his own judgment of excellence was well illustrated by his comments a few days after Ronnie's record had been unleashed on the markets of America and Britain. He was convinced that it would be a giant smash. Asked if it weren't a little too strange for the current record-buying public, he responded, "Too *strange?*"—

ly not understanding what was meant. After all, it wasn't a bit strange to *him*. Why shouldn't anyone else find it perfectly natural? He was absolutely right. One of these days somebody will call it a classic, and original pressings will be going for ten dollars down on Bleecker Street.

The rhythm section on that record included, by the way, George on guitar (who also made production suggestions), Leon Russell on piano (shades of olden days), Klaus Voorman on bass, and Jim Gordon, the former LA sessionman, on drums. It was cut in London. The B side, by the same performers, featured a friendly impromptu rocker called "Tandoori Chicken." "Tandoori" is the name

Ronnie
Spector

TRY SOME,
BUY SOME

Apple
33

of an Indian restaurant in London. The song came about when Phil sent someone out to get him some food from there. It is an indication of prevailing trends that some British radio stations actually played that instead of "Try Some." Phil plays the bluesy piano on this B side—and lying somewhere around the Apple offices is also a tape of him taking the lead vocal on the song. Once a Teddy Bear. . . .

The Next Great Event was Bangla Desh. George's great friend and former sitar tutor Ravi Shankar described for the ex-Beatle the civil war going on in his home country, and the mass of starving refugees it had spawned. George was moved to write "Bangla Desh," appealing for help for the people of East Pakistan. The song was released July 26, 1971. George announced that all his royalties from the record would go to a special Harrison/Shankar Relief Fund, c/o UNICEF. George put a lot of feeling into the record. His voice takes on unusually sad inflections—at times he's almost unrecognizable—and Spector backed him well with leaping riffs fortified by a grunting baritone sax. The B side, another "down" number, was an acoustic thing called "Deep Blue." It sounds like a jug band playing at a funeral. George sings very confidently, feeling no need to bury his voice in waves of production. His bottleneck work is beautifully restrained.

But it wasn't enough, so George organized probably the greatest rock concert of all time to take place at Madison Square Garden in New York on August 1. It was all in aid of Bangla Desh—by doing two shows, in the afternoon and evening, he contrived to raise about 260,000 dollars for the refugees. On the bill were George, Ringo, Leon Russell, Billy Preston, Eric Clapton, Jesse Davis, Klaus Voorman, Jim Keltner, Jim Horn, a choir and a horn section . . . and Bob Dylan, whose appearance no one could quite believe until it was over.

Behind the stage, Spector was watching the dials on Wally Heider's mobile 16-track recorder. Every note was preserved for posterity. George and Phil spent a week of nights at the Record Plant in New York, mixing it all down and selecting tracks for a three-record album. After they had finished, George took Dylan's side down to the poet's house in the Village, so he could hear it and give his consent for release.

Oh yes . . . and off to the side of the stage, during practically every number at the concert, were the four acoustic guitarists from Badfinger, strumming lightly on the beat. Even at Harrison's gig, Spector's influence was evident.

The Bangla Desh album, promised for release a week or two after the concert, was delayed for months by problems with the complex cover art work. In the meantime, rumors leaked about a new John Lennon album. Most of them said that it was the best thing he'd done in years.

The new album, *Imagine*, was softer and lusher in texture than *John Lennon/Plastic Ono Band*, and it represented a slight return to overt melodicism. John's comment: "There's less tension, lyric-wise and me-wise. We did something simple, like the previous album, but added simple strings over it, with the same attitude to the strings that we had towards the basic tracks on the *Plastic Ono Band* album."

It's the strings that give the album its distinctive texture, whether soothing and slightly creamy as on the ballads "Jealous Guy" and "How?", or tough and unsyrupy, as on "How Do You Sleep?"—the track built around a now legendary broadside at McCartney's supposed deficiencies in character and talent. The strings on that one are extraordinary: their little Moorish figures sound more like a single English horn than a load of violins, ending each phrase with a downward smear, cut off sharp like the guitars on "Cold Turkey." The effect is eerie. Elsewhere comes more brilliant use of instrumental resources, like the roaring tenor sax of the late King Curtis on "It's So Hard" and "I Don't Wanna Be A Soldier." Both Spector and Lennon had enormous admiration for the man whose tenor break on "Yakety Yak" and countless other R & B hits set a whole style into motion. (These tracks were recorded just a few weeks before Curtis's appalling murder in New York.)

George Harrison's solos on "How Do You Sleep?" and "Gimme Some Truth" could never be bettered. Lennon's voice fills with wonderment when he says: "Would you believe that George wasn't happy with these solos? He wanted to do them again! I told him that he'd never get 'em any better if he tried for years. It's the best he's played in his life, but he'd go on for ever if you let him."

For the strings on this album, Phil used a technique of overdubbing he remembered from old records, but which was new to Lennon: lay down the basic rhythm track, make a satisfactory rough mix immediately, then simply put the strings on another track. "It's just like adding to a finished record," John says. "It works well." Apart from questions of balance, it allowed them to get an idea of what they were doing earlier. As often as not the rough mix they made during the night of the session was the one which ended up on the record. "If you do it the same night, you're still in the mood of the take, and you remix it in that style. It often has the best feel, although some things aren't technically perfect. When you come back to it later and remix it technically, you might get a better sound but you might also lose the feel. I'd sooner have feeling than perfection, so would Yoko, and Phil's the same.

We get on really well, and that's why we call ourselves the Three Musketeers. It's a great partnership."

Danny Davis made the remark in late '71: "I can't conceive of guys as talented as the Beatles letting Phil take a full hand on the production of their albums. Phil is a great mixologist, to coin a phrase, and I figure that's his function in there. He mixes the records.

"There's no selling Phil short, but the feeling around the industry is that until the Beatles gave him a second chance, he'd just about had it."

Perhaps Lennon should have the last word on that:

"Phil's had the same kind of prejudice thrown at him that Yoko has, because they've both gone and touched the precious Beatles. And it's a load of crap . . . he's a real true genius. He was first in many fields, and he's still great. Apple's very lucky to have the best producer in the rock and roll world."

CODA
" ... good, and moving, and important...."

NOW THAT IT'S OVER, THOSE ARE THE WORDS that ring inside my head. Phil Spector wasn't, of course, the first person to make rock and roll records to which those adjectives apply. Nor will he be the last. But he was one of the few people, perhaps the only one, who ever *tried* to create music with such intentions, *and* still managed to make the result into good pop music.

His records can be approached on so many levels—his phrase sums it all up so well. "Good" because they were produced with imagination and a technical dexterity unknown until he came along; "moving" because he never forgot the roots of the music, in the Teenagers and the Crows and the Elegants, that first of all the music has to *speak* to people without any real conscious effort to hear; and "important" because he changed the whole sound of pop, and altered the world's attitude to the men who actually make the records.

If you've got this far, you may still be asking: so what *was* the Spector sound? How did he actually make that noise? As Tony Orlando says, "Everybody claims to know, but no one really does." I believe that the technical components of his production style are not difficult to understand. There's the crucial concentration on tape echo, culled from the Sun records, which alters the sound of every voice and instrument. Beyond that it's just a question of Spector's own ear, of knowing exactly when the echo and the mix are right. That's something which just can't be explained.

His musical evolution is the classic process of synthesis and development. His work stretches in an unbroken line right from the crude beginnings with the Teddy Bears to the complex webs of sound on *All Things Must Pass*. There's no reason to suspect that he won't go on refining his approach and dazzling us all. At the Lennon session, which could so easily have been an anticlimax, I truly felt in the presence of genius. As a creative power in pop, Spector is far from the burned out shell many people seem to think.

I'm not going to pretend this book is the last word on Spector, the definitive study. For every one person I spoke to, there are twenty more with good tales to tell—I hope somebody will get around to collecting them. But already, after less than a decade in some cases, memories have been wiped as clean as magnetic tape—partly because few people at the time suspected that what he was doing was "important," though it was obviously "good and moving." Those were simpler times; the idea of someone coming along and writing a book about it would have seemed preposterous. So some periods of his career are likely to remain forever lost to the chronicler.

What I hope this book does is send you back to your pile of singles, or down to an oldies shop, to search through piles of junked 45's for those rare gems he's given us over the years. In the end, I suppose it's the "moving" bit that counts for most, and his records have moved me more than pretty much anything else. It's the sound I grew up to; it marked my life, and if you're lucky it marked yours too. What can I say to him, except "Thank you?"

Richard Williams
London, December 1, 1971

NOTES

Chapter Three

(1) Phil Spector, interviewed in John Gillerland's radio series, *The Pop Chronicles*.
(2) Tom Wolfe: *The First Tycoon Of Teen* (part of *The Kandy-Kolored Tangerine-Flake Streamline Baby*, 1965).

Chapter Four

(1) Bill Millar: *The Drifters* (Studio Vista Rockbooks, 1971).
(2) *The Pop Chronicles*
(3) *Ibid*.

Chapter Six

(1) *Rolling Stone*, October 14, 1971.
(2) *Melody Maker*, October 11 and 18, 1969.
(3) *Fusion*, March 20, 1970.
(4) *Rolling Stone* (as above).
(5) *Melody Maker* (as above).
(6) *Melody Maker* (as above).

APPENDIX 1
PHIL SPECTOR DISCOGRAPHY

(Figures in parentheses identify date of entry to *Billboard* Hot 100, and highest position reached. [Courtesy *Record Research*, by Joel Whitburn])

PART A: PRE-PHILLES
TEDDY BEARS
"To Know Him Is To Love Him"/"Don't You Worry My Little Pet" (Dore 503) (9.28.58/1)
"Wonderful Lovable You"/"Till You're Mine" (Dore 520) (—)
"Oh Why"/"I Don't Need You Any More" (Imperial 5562) (3.15.59/91—2.22.59/98)
"If You Only Knew (The Love I Have For You)"/"You Said Goodbye" (Imperial 5581) (—)
"Don't Go Away"/"Seven Lonely Days" (Imperial 5594) (—)
The Teddy Bears Sing! (Imperial LP9067) Tracks:
"Oh Why," "Unchained Melody," "My Foolish Heart," "You Said Goodbye," "True Love," "Little Things Mean A Lot," "I Don't Need You Any More," "Tammy," "Long Ago And Far Away," "Don't Go Away," "If I Give My Heart To You," "Seven Lonely Days."
SPECTORS THREE
"I Really Do"/"I Know Why" (Trey 3001) (—)
"My Heart Stood Still"/"Mr. Robin" (Trey 3005) (—)
RAY PETERSON
"Corinna Corinna"/"Be My Girl" (Dunes 2002) (11.27.60/9)

CURTIS LEE
"Pretty Little Angel Eyes"/"Gee How I Wish You Were Here"
(Dunes 2007) (7.9.61/7)
"Under The Moon Of Love"/"Beverly Jean" (Dunes 2008)
(10.22.61/46)
PARIS SISTERS
"I Love How You Love Me" (Gregmark 6) (9.10.61/5)
"He Knows I Love Him Too Much" (Gregmark 10)
(1.27.62/34)
GENE PITNEY
"Every Breath I Take"/"Dream For Sale" (Musicor 1011)
(8.13.61/42)
CONNIE FRANCIS
"Second-Hand Love" (MGM 13074) (5.12.62/7)
RAY SHARPE
"Hey Little Girl"/"The Day You Left Me" (Garex)

PART B: PHILLES
(*—Not produced by Phil Spector)
PHILLES 45's

100   CRYSTALS: "There's No Other (Like My Baby)"/"Oh
Yeah, Maybe Baby" (11.26.61/20)
101   JOLLY SCOTT: "Here I Stand"/"You're My Only Love"
(—)*
102   CRYSTALS: "Uptown"/"What a Nice Way to Turn Seventeen" (3.31.62/13)
103   ALI HASSAN: "Chopsticks"/"Malaguena" (—)*
104   This number allocated to "Lt. Col. Bogey's Parade"—apparently unissued.*
105   CRYSTALS: "He Hit Me"/"No One Ever Tells You"
(released 7.21.62—withdrawn)
106   CRYSTALS: "He's a Rebel"/"I Love You Eddie" (9.8.62/1)
107   BOB B. SOXX AND THE BLUE JEANS: "Zip-
A-Dee-Doo-Dah"/"Flip and Nitty" (11.17.62/8)
108   ALLEY CATS: "Puddin N' Tain"/"Feel So Good"
(1.12.63/43)

109 CRYSTALS: "He's Sure The Boy I Love"/"Walkin' Along (La-La-La)" (12.29.62/11)
110 BOB B. SOXX AND THE BLUE JEANS: "Why Do Lovers Break Each Other's Heart"/"Dr. Kaplan's Office" (2.16.63/38)
111 DARLENE LOVE: "(Today I Met) The Boy I'm Gonna Marry"/"My Heart Beat A Little Bit Faster" (4.6.63/39)
112 CRYSTALS: "Da Doo Ron Ron"/"Git It" (4.27.63/3)
113 BOB B. SOXX AND THE BLUE JEANS: "Not Too Young to Get Married"/"Annette" (6.8.63/63)
114 DARLENE LOVE: "Wait 'Til My Bobby Gets Home"/"Take It From Me" (7.20.63/26)
115 CRYSTALS: "Then He Kissed Me"/"Brother Julius" (8.17.63/6)
116 RONETTES: "Be My Baby"/"Tedesco and Pitman" (8.31.63/2)
117 DARLENE LOVE: "A Fine, Fine Boy"/"Nino and Sonny (Big Trouble)" (10.19.63/53)
118 RONETTES: "Baby I Love You"/"Miss Joan and Mr. Sam" (12.21.63/24)
119 DARLENE LOVE: "Christmas (Baby Please Come Home)"/"Harry and Milt Meet Hal B." (released November 1963)
119 CRYSTALS: "Little Boy"/"Harry (from West Va.) and Milt" (2.1.64/92)
120 RONETTES: "(The Best Part of) Breakin' Up"/"Big Red" (4.4.64/39)
121 RONETTES: "Do I Love You"/"Bebe and Susu" (6.20.64/34)
122 CRYSTALS: "All Grown Up"/"Irving (Jaggered Sixteenths)" (8.1.64/98)
123 DARLENE LOVE: "Stumbled and Fell"/"He's a Quiet Guy" (unreleased; catalogue number given to Ronettes)
123 RONETTES: "Walkin' In The Rain"/"How Does It Feel?" (10.24.64/23)
124 RIGHTEOUS BROTHERS: "You've Lost That Lovin' Feelin'"/"There's a Woman" (12.2.64/1)

125   DARLENE LOVE: "Christmas (Baby Please Come Home)"/"Winter Wonderland" (released November 1964)

126   RONETTES: "Born to Be Together"/"Blues for Baby" (2.6.65/52)

127   RIGHTEOUS BROTHERS: "Just Once in My Life"/"The Blues" (4.10.65/9)

128   RONETTES: "Oh I Love You"/"Is This What I Get for Loving You?" (5.29.65/75)

129   RIGHTEOUS BROTHERS: "Unchained Melody"/"Hung on You" (7.17.65/4-47)

130   RIGHTEOUS BROTHERS: "Ebb Tide"/"(I Love You) for Sentimental Reasons" (12.4.65/5)

131   IKE AND TINA TURNER: "River Deep—Mountain High"/"I'll Keep You Happy" (5.29.66/88)

132   RIGHTEOUS BROTHERS: "The White Cliffs of Dover"/"She's Mine, All Mine" (—)

133   RONETTES: "I Can Hear Music"*/"When I Saw You" (10.29.66/100)

134   IKE AND TINA TURNER: "A Man Is a Man Is a Man"/"Two to Tango" (unreleased)

135   IKE AND TINA TURNER: "I'll Never Need More Than This"/"The Cashbox Blues" (unreleased)

136   IKE AND TINA TURNER: "A Love like Yours (Don't Come Knocking Every Day)"/"I Idolize You" (unreleased)

The following records on the British London label feature tracks not similarly released in America:

HL 9725   DARLENE LOVE: "(Today I Met) The Boy I'm Gonna Marry"/"Playing For Keeps" (1963)

HLU 9852   CRYSTALS: "I Wonder"/"Little Boy" (1964)

HLU 10083   IKE AND TINA TURNER: "A Love like Yours (Don't Come Knocking Every Day)"/"Hold On Baby" (1966)

HLU 10155   IKE AND TINA TURNER: "I'll Never Need More Than This"/"Save the Last Dance for Me" (1967)

PHILLES ALBUMS

PHLP 4000   CRYSTALS: *Twist Uptown*. Tracks: "Uptown," "Another Country—Another World," "Frankenstein Twist,"

"Oh Yeah, Maybe Baby," "Please Hurt Me," "There's No Other (Like My Baby)," "On Broadway," "What a Nice Way to Turn Seventeen," "No One Ever Tells You," "Gee Whiz Look at His Eyes (Twist)," "I Love You Eddie." (1962)

PHLP 4001 CRYSTALS: *He's a Rebel.* Tracks: "He's a Rebel," "Uptown," "Another Country—Another World," "Frankenstein Twist," "Oh Yeah, Maybe Baby," "He's Sure the Boy I Love," "There's No Other (Like My Baby)," "On Broadway," "What a Nice Way to Turn Seventeen," "No One Ever Tells You," "He Hit Me," "I Love You Eddie." (1963)

PHLP 4002 BOB B. SOXX AND THE BLUE JEANS: *Zip-Zip-A-Dee-Doo-Dah.* Tracks: "'Zip-A-Dee-Doo-Dah," "Why Do Lovers Break Each Other's Heart, "Let the Good Times Roll," "My Heart Beat a Little Bit Faster," "Jimmy Baby," "Baby (I Love You)," "The White Cliffs of Dover," "This Land Is Your Land," "Dear (Here Comes My Baby)," "I Shook the World," "Everything's Gonna Be All Right," "Dr. Kaplan's Office." (1963)

PHLP 4003 CRYSTALS: *The Crystals Sing the Greatest Hits, Volume I.* Tracks: "Da Doo Ron Ron," "On Broadway," "He's A Rebel," "Hot Pastrami," "There's No Other (Like My Baby)," "The Wah Watusi," "Mashed Potato Time," "He's Sure the Boy I Love," "Uptown," "The Twist," "Gee Whiz (Look at His Eyes)," "Look in My Eyes." (1963)

PHLP 4004 *Philles Records Presents Today's Hits.* Tracks: "Then He Kissed Me," "Da Doo Ron Ron," "Oh Yeah, Maybe Baby" (CRYSTALS); "Zip-A-Dee-Doo-Dah," "Why Do Lovers Break Each Other's Heart," "Not Too Young to Get Married," (BOB B. SOXX AND THE BLUE JEANS); "Be My Baby" (RONETTES); "Wait 'Til My Bobby Gets Home," "(Today I Met) The Boy I'm Gonna Marry," "My Heart Beat a Little Bit Faster," "Playing for Keeps" (DARLENE LOVE); "Puddin N' Tain" (ALLEY CATS). (1963)

PHLP 4005 *A Christmas Gift For You.* Tracks: "White Christmas," "(It's a) Marshmallow World," "Winter Wonderland," "Christmas (Baby Please Come Home)" (DARLENE LOVE);

"Frosty the Snowman," "Sleigh Ride," "I Saw Mommy Kissing Santa Claus" (RONETTES); "The Bells of St. Mary," "Here Comes Santa Claus" (BOB B. SOXX AND THE BLUE JEANS); "Santa Claus Is Comin' To Town," "Rudolph The Red Nosed Reindeer," "Parade of the Wooden Soldiers" (CRYSTALS); "Silent Night" (PHIL SPECTOR AND ARTISTS). (1963)

PHLP 4006 RONETTES: *Presenting the Fabulous Ronettes, Featuring Veronica*. Tracks: "Walkin' In the Rain," "Do I Love You," "So Young," "(The Best Part Of) Breakin' Up," "I Wonder," "What'd I Say," "Be My Baby," "You Baby," "Baby I Love You," "How Does It Feel?", "When I Saw You," "Chapel of Love." (1964)

PHLP 4007 RIGHTEOUS BROTHERS: *You've Lost That Lovin' Feelin'*. Tracks: "You've Lost That Lovin' Feelin'," "Ko Ko Mo," "Ol' Man River," "Look At Me," "What'd I Say," "The Angels Listened In," "Sick and Tired," "Summertime," "Over And Over," "Soul City," "There's A Woman."

PHLP 4008 RIGHTEOUS BROTHERS: *Just Once in My Life*. Tracks: "Just Once in My Life," "Big Boy Pete," "Unchained Melody," "You Are My Sunshine," "The Great Pretender," "Sticks and Stones," "See That Girl," "Oo-Poo-Pah-Doo," "You'll Never Walk Alone," "Guess Who?", "The Blues." (1965)

PHLP 4009 RIGHTEOUS BROTHERS: *Back To Back*. Tracks: "Ebb Tide," "God Bless the Child," "Hot Tamales," "Hallelujah I Love Her So," "She's Mine, All Mine," "Hung on You," "For Sentimental Reasons," "White Cliffs of Dover," "Loving You," "Without a Doubt," "Late Late Night." (1965)

PHLP 4010 IKE AND TINA TURNER: *River Deep–Mountain High*. Tracks: "River Deep—Mountain High," "I Idolize You," "A Love Like Yours (Don't Come Knocking Every Day)," "A Fool in Love," "Make 'Em Wait," "Hold on Baby," "Save the Last Dance for Me," "Oh Baby! (Things Ain't What They Used to Be)," "Every Day I Have to Cry," "Such a Fool for You," "It's Gonna Work out Fine," "You're So Fine." (Unissued in America, but released in Britain as London HAU 8298, 1966)

PART C: PHIL SPECTOR RECORDS, ANNETTE, PHI-DAN

PHIL SPECTOR RECORDS

1   IMAGINATIONS: "Hold Me Tight" (Believed issued in March, 1964)
2   VERONICA: "Why Don't They Let Us Fall In Love?"/"Chubby Danny D" (Released regionally 7.2.64; never released nationally)

ANNETTE

1001   BONNIE JO MASON: "I Love You, Ringo" (Limited regional release)
1002   HARVEY AND DOC AND THE DWELLERS: "Uncle Kev"/"Oh Baby"

PHI-DAN

5000   FLORENCE DeVORE: "Kiss Me Now"/"We're Not Old Enough"
5001   BETTY WILLIS: "Act Naturally"
5002   BONNIE AND THE TREASURES: "Home of the Brave"/"Our Song" (8.28.65/77)

PART D: A & M

A & M 45's

1039   CHECKMATES LTD.: "Love Is All I Have to Give"/"Never Should Have Tried" (4.5.69/65)
1040   RONETTES featuring The Voice of Veronica: "You Came, You Saw, You Conquered"/"I Can Hear Music" (Released in March, 1969)
1053   SONNY CHARLES AND THE CHECKMATES LTD.: "Black Pearl"/"Lazy Susan" (5.10.69/13)
1127   SONNY CHARLES AND THE CHECKMATES LTD.: "Proud Mary"/"Do You Love Your Baby" (10.18.69/69)

A & M ALBUMS

SP4183   CHECKMATES LTD.: *Love Is All We Have to Give.* Tracks: "Proud Mary," "Spanish Harlem," "Black Pearl,"

"I Keep Forgettin'," "Love Is All I Have to Give," "The *Hair* Anthology Suite." (Released 9.13.69)

SP4178 IKE AND TINA TURNER: *River Deep–Mountain High.* Tracks as Philles PHLP 4010, but "I'll Never Need More than This" replaces "You're So Fine." (Released 9.13.69)

PART E: APPLE

APPLE 45's

1818   JOHN LENNON/PLASTIC ONO BAND: "Instant Karma"/"Who Has Seen the Wind" (released 2.9.70)

2995   GEORGE HARRISON: "My Sweet Lord"/"Isn't It a Pity" (11.13.70)

1828   GEORGE HARRISON: "What Is Life"/"Apple Scruffs" (2.8.71)

1830   JOHN LENNON/PLASTIC ONO BAND: "Power to the People"/"Touch Me" (3.20.71)

1832   RONNIE SPECTOR: "Try Some, Buy Some"/"Tandoori Chicken" (4.12.71)

1836   GEORGE HARRISON: "Bangla Desh"/"Deep Blue" (7.26.71)

1840   JOHN LENNON: "Imagine"/"It's So Hard" (9.27.71)

1843   JOHN LENNON/YOKO ONO: "Happy Xmas (War Is Over)"/"Snow Is Falling" (12.11.71)

APPLE ALBUMS

AR 34001 THE BEATLES: *Let It Be.* Tracks: "Two Of Us," "Dig a Pony," "Across the Universe," "I Me Mine," "Dig It," "Let It Be," "Maggie May," "I've Got a Feeling," "One After 909," "The Long and Winding Road," "For You Blue," "Get Back." (Released 5.5.70)

STCH 639 GEORGE HARRISON: *All Things Must Pass.* Tracks: "I'd Have You Anytime," "My Sweet Lord," "Wah Wah," "Isn't It a Pity," "What Is Life," "If Not for You," "Behind That Locked Door," "Let It Down," "Run of the Mill," "Beware of Darkness," "Apple Scruffs," "Ballad of Sir Frankie Crisp (Let It Roll)," "Awaiting on You All,"

"All Things Must Pass," "I Dig Love," "Art of Dying," "Isn't It a Pity," "Hear Me Lord," "Out of the Blue," "It's Johnny's Birthday," "Plug Me In," "I Remember Jeep," "Thanks for the Pepperoni." (Released 11.27.70).

SW 3372 JOHN LENNON: *John Lennon/Plastic Ono Band.* Tracks: "Mother," "Hold on John," "I Found Out," "Working Class Hero," "Isolation," "Remember," "Love," "Well Well Well," "Look at Me," "God," "My Mummy's Dead." (Released 12.7.70)

SW 3379 JOHN LENNON: *Imagine.* Tracks: "Imagine," "Crippled Inside," "Jealous Guy," "It's So Hard," "I Don't Wanna Be a Soldier Mama I Don't Wanna Die," "Gimme Some Truth," "Oh My Love," "How Do Yo Sleep?","How?", "Oh Yoko!" (Released 9.13.71)

APPENDIX 2
WHERE ARE THEY NOW?

LOU ADLER

Adler managed Jan and Dean and Johnny Rivers, and then formed the Dunhill label, on which he produced the Mama's and the Papa's. He's now a millionaire, owns the Ode label, and manages Carole King. A very clever man, he's been at the center of the whole West Coast sound.

JEFF BARRY

Jeff and Ellie separated long ago, and although Ellie is still writing, it's Jeff who's become America's top producer of Bubblegum and allied forms of music. Since Spector, he's recorded the Dixie Cups, the Shangri-Las, the Monkees, the Archies, Andy Kim, Neil Diamond, Bobby Bloom, and Dusty Springfield. That's what you call a track record. In 1971, he was also very involved in the New York production of *The Dirtiest Show In Town.*

DANNY DAVIS

On leaving Spector in 1966, Danny stayed in Los Angeles and now works for Columbia/Screen Gems.

LEE HAZLEWOOD

Hazlewood was the man who put Nancy Sinatra into those boots that were made for walking, and he's been responsible for almost all of her records—including the superb duets they cut together on his own unorthodox songs, like "Some Velvet Morning" and "Sand." Don't sneer—listen to 'em.

CAROLE KING

The British invasion hit Carole and Gerry Goffin quite hard, because it soon became the fashion for groups to write their own songs, and professional composers went out of style. However, she returned, minus Gerry, in 1970, and was at the top of the charts for most of the next year with a fine album called *Tapestry*. She'd befriended James Taylor, and had adopted the new, understated mode of delivery. She's now married to Charlie Larkey, the bass player with Jo Mama, and still writes great songs.

DONNY KIRSHNER

Kirshner sold Aldon Music to Screen Gems in the Sixties, and with it went all his writers. He set up a new company, Kirshner Entertainment Corporation, and is now one of the moguls of the leisure industry.

LEIBER AND STOLLER

With George Goldner, they formed the Red Bird label around '64, and had an amazing string of hits with the Shangri-Las, Dixie Cups, Jelly Beans, Tradewinds, Ad Libs, and others. But the label folded, for reasons no one is prepared to put a name to, and they went into semi-retirement. Only in 1971 did they re-emerge, having bought the King/Starday company in association with two other people, and their first shot was a remake of "Love Potion No. 9," with the Coasters. They'd first made the song a hit for the Clovers, back in '59. Now, thank goodness, Jerry and Mike are again spending most of their time in the studios.

GEORGE GOLDNER

Goldner had apparently lost a fortune by the time he went into Red Bird with Leiber and Stoller. In 1969 he formed the Firebird label, but nothing much came out of it and he died on April 15, 1970, aged 52. Bill Millar's obituary is the best tribute: "He was the original Fifties Bubblegum king, without a mind for stone Blues. Nor was he entirely punctilious over royalty payments. But he cut some nice records, and he did more for integration than the Supreme Court."

BARRY MANN

He and his wife carried on writing successfully, all through the Sixties, and Barry made a surprise reappearance, late in '71, with a solo album for Columbia.

TONY ORLANDO

After a long period in the publishing business, when his early career as a singer had faded, Orlando fell, virtually by accident, back into performing. He's now the unmistakably Ben E. King-influenced lead voice of Dawn, who have had several giant Top 40 smashes: "Candida" (Ben E. turned that song down because he thought it "too old fashioned"), "Knock Three Times," and "What Are You Doing Sunday?".

LESTER SILL

For the past five or six years he's been the boss of Screen Gems, based on the West Coast.

APPENDIX 3
SONGS

The following is tabulation of songs which Spector composed, alone and in collaboration with others.

SPECTOR
"To Know Him Is To Love Him," "Don't You Worry My Little Pet," "Wonderful Lovable You," "Till You're Mine," "You Said Goodbye," "Don't Go Away," "If You Only Knew (The Love I Have for You)," "Oh Why," "I Don't Need You Any More," "I Really Do," "I Know Why," "Mr. Robin," "Baby (I Love You)," "Everything's Gonna Be Alright," "Dear (Here Comes My Baby)," "When I Saw You," "I'll Keep You Happy," "Tandoori Chicken."

LEIBER/SPECTOR
"Spanish Harlem."

SPECTOR/POMUS
"First Taste of Love," "Young Boy Blues," "Another Country—Another World."

SPECTOR/HUNTER
"Second-Hand Love," "Oh Yeah, Maybe Baby," "I Love You Eddie."

SPECTOR/SANDS
"Be My Girl," "Take It From Me," "Playing for Keeps" (N.B.: Spector says that "Sands" is a made-up name.)

SPECTOR/PHILLIPS
"Dream for Sale."

SPECTOR/BATES
"There's No Other (Like My Baby)."

SPECTOR/KING/GOFFIN
"No One Ever Tells You," "Just Once in My Life," "Hung on You."

SPECTOR/MANN/WEIL
"You've Lost That Lovin' Feelin'," "You Baby," "Walking In The Rain."

SPECTOR/GREENWICH/POWERS
"Why Do Lovers Break Each Other's Heart," "My Heart Beat a Little Bit Faster," "(Today I Met) The Boy I'm Gonna Marry."

SPECTOR/BARRY/GREENWICH
"Da Doo Ron Ron," "Then He Kissed Me," "Be My Baby," "Wait 'Til My Bobby Gets Home," "A Fine, Fine Boy," "Baby I Love You," "Not Too Young To Get Married," "Little Boy," "I Wonder," "All Grown Up," "Chapel of Love," "Christmas (Baby Please Come Home)," "Why Don't They Let Us Fall in Love," "I Can Hear Music," "River Deep—Mountain High," "I'll Never Need More than This."

SPECTOR/PONCIA/ANDREOLI
"(The Best Part of) Breakin' Up," "Do I Love You," "How Does It Feel?"

SPECTOR/PHELGE
"Little By Little" (N.B.: "Nanker/Phelge" was a compositional pseudonym used by Mick Jagger and Keith Richard.)

SPECTOR/WINE/LEVINE
"You Came, You Saw, You Conquered," "Black Pearl," "I Love You like I Love My Very Life" (N.B.: The latter song was recorded by Carla Thomas, on Stax 0080.)

SPECTOR/STEVENS
"Love Is All I Have to Give."

MANN/WEIL alone wrote "Home Of The Brave," "He's Sure The Boy I Love," and "Uptown." MANN/KOLBER wrote "I

Love How You Love Me." GOFFIN/KING wrote "Every Breath
I Take," "He Hit Me," "Please Hurt Me," "He Knows I Love
Him Too Much." GENE PITNEY wrote "He's a Rebel."
GREENWICH/BARRY wrote "Hold On Baby."

INDEX